THE COMMEMORATIVE MEDAL
ITS APPRECIATION AND COLLECTION

THE COMMEMORATIVE MEDAL

ITS APPRECIATION AND COLLECTION

HOWARD W. A. LINECAR
FRNS FRSA NLG

GALE RESEARCH COMPANY
BOOK TOWER, DETROIT, MICHIGAN 48226

First published in 1974 in the United States
by the Gale Research Company, Book Tower, Detroit 48226

Linecar, Howard W A 1912—
    The commemorative medal.
    Library of Congress
    Cataloguing in Publication Data
    1. Medals.   I. Title.
CJ5725.L54   737'.2   72-12989
ISBN 0-8103-2012-6

© Howard W. A. Linecar 1974

All rights reserved. No part of this
publication may be reproduced, stored
in a retrieval system, or transmitted,
in any form or by any means, electronic,
mechanical, photocopying, recording or
otherwise without the prior permission
of the Gale Research Company

Printed in Great Britain

CONTENTS

		page
	List of Illustrations	7
	Acknowledgements	11
	Introduction	15
	The Plates	17
1	The Medal as an Art Form—Its History	51
2	The Medal in Britain—Sixteenth to Eighteenth Centuries	61
3	The Industrial Revolution and the Medal	73
4	The Medal in the Twentieth Century—Its Return to an Art Form	83
5	The Medal Overseas	95
6	The Medal as a Collector's Piece	103
7	Collecting Themes	115
	Appendices	
	I An Example of Thematic Collection	127
	II Sources of Further Information	141
	Index	151

LIST OF ILLUSTRATIONS

	page
PLATE I	18

1. Greek silver decadrachm
2. Roman bronze as
3. Bronze coin celebrating Rome's 900th anniversary
4. Gold coin of Diocletian
5. Gold medallion of Constantius I Chlorus
6. Medal depicting Lucrezia Borgia
7. Plastic medal commemorating Romney, Hythe & Dymchurch Railway

PLATE II	20

1. Gold solidus of Theodoric
2. 'Portrait' of William Shakespeare
3. Silver medal commemorating John Colet
4. Cast lead medal of James IV of Scotland
5. Cast bronze medal of Sir Thomas More
6. Bronze medal of Myles Coverdale
7. Cast bronze medal of Pope Paul III
8. Silver medal of Henry VIII as head of the Church
9. Edward VI coronation medal
10. Nineteenth-century medal commemorating Edward VI

PLATE III	22

1. Bronze medal showing Birmingham Free Grammar School
2. Medal commemorating Lady Jane Grey

7

LIST OF ILLUSTRATIONS

page

3   Bronze medal of Mary Queen of Scots
4   Silver Medal of Mary Queen of Scots
5   Silver medal of Philip of Spain and Mary
6   Medal commemorating accession of Elizabeth I
7   Medal celebrating the defeat of the Spanish Armada
8   Dangers Averted, 1589

PLATE IV   24

1   Royalist badge of Charles I
2   The Dunbar Medal, 1650
3   Naval reward medal, 1665
4   Medal celebrating British colonisation, 1670
5   Naval reward medal of James II

PLATE V   26

1   French medal celebrating Louis XIV and Philip of Anjou
2   Portrait of Louis XIV
3   Treaty of Passarowitz, 1718
4   Medal commemorating death of 1st Duke of Marlborough
5   George II coronation medal
6   Medal celebrating Frederick, Prince of Wales, 1729
7   Medal celebrating marriage of Prince of Orange and Princess Anne, 1734

PLATE VI   28

1   Memorial medal to Matthew Boulton
2   Memorial medal to James Watt
3   Presentation medal for participants in Battle of Trafalgar
4   Medal celebrating first underwater tunnel
5   Celebratory medal on opening of Liverpool & Manchester Railway
6   Medal showing Stephenson locomotive
7   Portrait of 1st Duke of Wellington

LIST OF ILLUSTRATIONS

PLATE VII — page 30
1. Medal celebrating Thomas Telford and the Menai Bridge
2. Medal celebrating opening of L & MR
3. Celebratory medal for opening of Grand Junction Railway
4. Depiction of Crystal Palace
5. Depiction of Alexandra Palace
6. Medal showing some of the work by Perrault on the Louvre, Paris

PLATE VIII — 32
1. William IV coronation miniature medal
2. Victoria coronation medal
3. Medal celebrating Queen Victoria's visit to Guildhall
4. Medal commemorating launching of *Great Britain*
5. Edward VII coronation medal
6. George V coronation medal
7. George VI coronation medal
8. Elizabeth II coronation crown

PLATE IX — 34
1. Medal celebrating opening of Tower Bridge
2. Investiture medal for Edward, Prince of Wales
3. World War I naval medal
4. Medal commemorating World War I bombardment of Scarborough
5. Unofficial victory medal, World War I
6. Silver medal commemorating Silver Jubilee of George V

PLATE X — 36
1. Art Union medal
2. Medal showing Lincoln Cathedral

LIST OF ILLUSTRATIONS

page

  3 Medal celebrating 200th anniversary of British Museum
  4 Churchill memorial medal

PLATE XI   38
1. Medal commemorating William Penn
2. Medal commemorating Lord Tennyson
3. Baden-Powell memorial medal
4. Royal Geographical Society medal, showing Dr Livingstone
5. RGS medal celebrating Sir Vivian Fuchs' trans-Antarctic expedition
6. Sanford Saltus medal
7. Henley Horticultural Society medal
8. Olympic medal, 1908

PLATE XII   40
1. Medal celebrating commissioning of *Queen Mary*
2. LMS medal commemorating London & Birmingham Railway
3. Medal commemorating Battle of Shrewsbury

PLATE XIII   42
1. Medal celebrating 400th anniversary of discovery of America
2. Modern medallic portrait of Tolstoy
3. French railway medal celebrating electrification

PLATE XIV   44
1. Modern medal of Louis XIV and Palace of Versailles
2. A final warning?

PLATE XV   46
    A purpose-built medal cabinet

PLATE XVI   47
    Medals displayed in a glass-topped showcase

ACKNOWLEDGEMENTS

Thanks are due to the Trustees of the British Museum for permission to reproduce the following medals: Plate I, nos 1–6; Plate II, nos 1–10; Plate III, nos 1–8; Plate IV, nos 1–5; Plate V, nos 1–7; Plate VI, nos 2–4 and 6–7; Plate VII, no 6; Plate VIII, nos 1–3 and 5–8; Plate IX, nos 2–4 and 6; Plate X, nos 1–4; Plate XI, nos 1–8; Plate XII, no 3; Plate XIII, nos 1–2; and Plate XIV, nos 1–2.

In particular thanks are due to Joan Martin of the Department of Coins and Medals, British Museum for her care and thought in selecting these medals from the great collection at her command.

Thanks are also due to Graham Pollard of the Fitzwilliam Museum, Cambridge, for his reading of the manuscript in its original form, and for his expert advice and suggestions.

DEDICATION

The Numismatic Literary Guild, founded in the United States of America, most generously awarded me life membership. It is a pleasure to dedicate this book to present and future members of this exclusive guild, as some small return for the honour conferred on me.

INTRODUCTION

INTRODUCTION

AS INTEREST in numismatics has widened on an unprecedented scale during the last twenty-five years the cost of coins has increased with the enlargement of the market. Leaving aside the richer collector and the more opulent investor in coins, many collectors and potential collectors have been looking around for some numismatic collecting theme that is within their means, and are taking up banknotes and commemorative medals.

The prices of medals fall between those of banknotes and the scarcer coins—not the rarer coins whose prices can be astronomical. I hope to show that the medal, though a quite separate collection subject from the coin—as is the banknote—can be of great interest to the collector. The coin, medal and banknote collectors are all basically interested in the background history of their subject. The coin collector, unless he is simply a speculator collecting as a hedge against inflation, may delve into obscure historic and economic problems of the period in which he is interested. Though his collecting theme, and coin-collecting themes are almost endless, he recreates some part of the period of history in which his coins were current. The banknote collector, a relative newcomer, is following a similar course. The commemorative medal, though not so ancient in its conception as the coin but older than the banknote, forms an equally rich collecting field; one which, until recently, has been left almost unexplored by the British collector. This book is, therefore, primarily written for him, though it should give some interest, help and information to collectors in countries where

INTRODUCTION

the medal has long been appreciated.

The commemorative medal may be defined as a medal manufactured to commemorate something of historical interest and importance, or some person or persons falling into the same category. From this point of view the medal seeks to be a direct mirror of history, if sometimes a distorting mirror, a purpose not intended for the coin. Campaign medals, war medals, civil medals and decorations, all designed to be worn on the person, though derived in part from the commemorative medal, are an entirely separate subject. Throughout this book, therefore, the word 'medal' means the commemorative medal, even though some of these have on occasion been worn on the person.

The lack of interest in the medal has arisen in part from the lack of standard reference works on the subject. This point will become clearer as the story proceeds. While work is in hand which will go some way to rectify this omission, there remains a large field of interesting research work open to the collector. He is also likely to find that his collection will appreciate in value as time goes on.

Since medal collecting is a very large subject, this book is not a catalogue. The illustrations are designed to show something of the history and appearance of medals, their purpose and the possibilities for the collector: they are therefore captioned at some length, as an adjunct to the main text. It is hoped that this book, coming at a moment when there is a rising appreciation of the British medal, may be of some help and guidance to those who would look further into a collecting theme of the widest possible interest.

THE PLATES

The coins and medals illustrated are either in the British Museum or are shown by courtesy of Spink & Son, Ltd.

PLATE I

1   Ancient Greece. Silver decadrachm, or ten-drachma piece, struck about 412 BC. Seltman in *Masterpieces of Greek Coinage* states that they were prize-coins for the Assinarian Games. Davis in *Greek Coins and Cities* suggests that pieces of this type, of which there are several varieties by different artists, may have been intended to celebrate the anniversaries of the victory of Syracuse over the Athenians in 413 BC. Either way these Syracusan coins were certainly commemorative. This specimen is signed by its artist KIMON, his initials being on the hair-band on Arethusa's forehead.
2   Rome. Cast bronze As (liberal standard). Demonstrating how large a coin can be, this example was in use after 235 BC. The obverse here shows the head of Janus.
3   Rome. One of the bronze coins struck by Antoninus Pius (AD 138–61) to commemorate the 900th anniversary of the foundation of Rome.
4   Rome. Gold coin struck by Diocletian (AD 284–95) after the reform of the coinage. The piece may have been intended for presentation purposes.
5   Rome. The gold medallion of Constantius I Chlorus (see p 53) Electrotype copy.
6   Lucrezia Borgia (1480–1519), wife of Alfonso I d'Este. An example of a cast Renaissance medal from Italy.
7   Compare all the above with a medal cast in man-made plastic, commemorating the fortieth year of the Romney, Hythe & Dymchurch Railway, 1927–67. Though the lettering is clear and sharp, the locomotive is poor in perspective and inaccurate in detail, but as a commemorative piece it served its purpose and was given gratis to passengers.

PLATE II

1 Italy. Unique triple gold solidus: portrait of Theodoric (AD 493–526). Reverse shows figure of Victory. Both sides have Theodoric's name. This contemporary portrait piece is still a coin. Electrotype copy, coin in the Berlin cabinet.

2 'Portrait' of William Shakespeare, struck in 1844, illustrating an after-the-event medal.

3 John Colet (1466–1519) the founder of St Paul's School in 1509. Engraved by G. F. Pigeon, a nineteenth-century medallist who worked for a time in Boulton's Soho Mint in Birmingham.

4 Obverse cast in lead, of James IV of Scotland; died 1513. Only the obverse exists in this metal. First supposed to be contemporary, and prepared when James was about to make his fatal invasion of England. Now thought to have been executed on the Continent, late sixteenth century or after. MI 1, 26/7.

5 Cast bronze, of Sir Thomas More, commemorating his execution on Tower Hill, 1535. Contemporary, in the coarse but expressive style of the period. MI 1, 34/23. Probably unique.

6 Obverse, bronze, of Myles Coverdale (1487–1568), translator of the Bible, 1535. By Davis, Birmingham, 1835. Reverse reads TO COMMEMORATE THAT GLORIOUS EVENT THE PUBLICATION OF THE FIRST ENGLISH BIBLE BY MYLES COVERDALE OCTR. 4th 1535 AND OF THE THIRD CENTURY OF THE PROTESTANT REFORMATION CELEBRATED OCTR. 4th, 1835. MI 1, 37/25.

7 Obverse, cast bronze, high relief, of Pope Paul III (1534–49) probably by Valerio Belli. May commemorate Henry VIII's excommunication in 1538, or the Pope's reduction of Perugia. MI 1 39/31.

8 Obverse, silver, 1545, after the proclamation of Henry VIII as head of the Church in 1535. The legend translates, HENRY VIII KING OF ENGLAND FRANCE AND IRELAND DEFENDER OF THE FAITH AND UNDER CHRIST THE SUPREME HEAD OF THE CHURCH OF ENGLAND AND IRELAND. MI 1, 47/45.

9 Obverse, silver, commemorating the coronation of Edward VI, 1547. The legend details his style and titles, ending, CROWNED 20 FEBRUARY 1546 (sic) AT THE AGE OF TEN YEARS. The legend is repeated on the reverse in Hebrew and Greek. Cast, or struck on cast metal and chased. The first coronation medal issued in England. MI 1, 53/1.

10 Obverse, nineteenth century, Edward VI. Sets of medals, all imaginative portraits, were issued at this period, of all the kings and queens of England. Struck in gold in limited numbers, silver and bronze, and sold as sets in book-form cases.

PLATE III

1 Reverse, bronze, Birmingham Free Grammar School, founded by Edward VI, 1552, as it appeared in 1836. Barry was the architect of the Houses of Parliament. Engraved by Joseph Davis, struck in 1852, Birmingham. MI 1, 59/11.

2 Lady Jane Grey (1537-54). The Duke of Northumberland, whose son married Jane Grey, induced Edward VI to alter the succession in her favour when the King was dying. Jane was proclaimed and reigned for eleven days. On the crown being transferred to Mary, eldest daughter of Henry VIII, Jane and her husband were beheaded at the Tower. Modern, made for Edward Emery (died circa 1850), a collector and coin dealer. Examples of coins looking like medals have been given. This medal was designed to look like a coin. MI 1, 63/1.

3 Bronze portrait by Tassie (1735-99) of Queen Mary Stuart (Mary Queen of Scots). One of an apparently uncompleted series of Scottish Sovereigns. From the recumbent figure of Mary in Westminster Abbey. Reverse gives important dates in the Queen's life. She was beheaded in 1587, age forty-four. MI 1, 139/98.

4 Obverse, silver, contemporary portrait of Mary Queen of Scots. May have been a pattern for a coin. Engraved by Acheson, Engraver to the Mint of Scotland, in 1553. MI 1, 65/4.

5 Philip and Mary (1554-8). Cast, silver, and chased, in high relief. Fine contemporary portraits. MI 1, 72/18.

6 Obverse, bronze, commemorating the accession of Elizabeth I, 1558. MI 1, 91/3.

7 Defeat of the Spanish Armada, 1588, in gold. The satirical obverse shows the Pope, kings, bishops and others in consultation, eyes bandaged, the floor covered in spikes. The legends translate OH! THE BLIND MINDS THE BLIND HEARTS OF MEN. IT IS HARD TO KICK AGAINST THE PRICKS (Acts, ix, 5). Reverse, a spirited scene, showing the Spanish fleet wrecked, with survivors. Low relief, contemporary. MI 1, 144/111.

8 Dangers Averted, 1589, cast, contemporary, in remarkably high relief and great detail. Possibly intended as a naval reward (see p 67). The portrait is one of the finest in any medium. Unsigned, thought to be by Nicholas Hilliard (1547-1619), goldsmith, jeweller, linmer and miniature painter. In gold and silver, the British Museum silver example has its original chain. MI 1, 154/129.

PLATE IV

1 Example of a Royalist Badge of Charles I, with his queen Henrietta Maria on the reverse. Most of these badges were made by joining two embossed plates back-to-back within a rim-type frame. They were made of gold, silver-gilt and silver, and are rare. MI 1, 353 ff.

2 The Dunbar Medal, 1650 (see p 68). Struck in gold silver and bronze. Specimens of the obverse alone are sometimes seen, struck later after the reverse die had apparently been lost. Later copies of the medal exist, but are valueless. MI 1, 391/13. Extremely rare.

3 A naval reward medal, 1665, not intended for wearing. Struck in gold and silver by John Roettier, one of Charles II's protégés, and originally given to those who showed outstanding conduct at the Battle of Lowestoft, with the rank of Captain and above. Purposely undated, it could be applicable for any similar purpose during the period of great trade rivalry and consequent fighting between the English and Dutch. The obverse has a good portrait of Charles, and the reverse shows him, habited as a Roman general, viewing a naval engagement. MI 1, 503/139.

4 British Colonisation, 1670. Designed by John Roettier and struck in gold and silver. The medal was once thought to allude to the dowry of Queen Catherine, which laid the foundation of the British Empire in India. More probably it refers to the colonies on the continent and islands of America, the warfare carried on against the piratical state of Barbary in Africa and the acquisition of territory in Asia. The contemporary map on the reverse is of great interest. Latitude and longitude and the equator appear, as against the criss-cross of lines seen on earlier maps. Science was advancing. Charles II sponsored the Royal Society, the world's leading scientific body, and also Greenwich Observatory, and appointed Flamsteed first Astronomer Royal. MI 1, 546/203.

5 Struck for similar purposes to those of medal 3, in gold and silver, in 1685, for James II. Engraved by John Roettier, whose initial is seen below the bust. MI 1, 617/29. The actual obverse die may be seen in the British Museum.

26

PLATE V

1 The War of the Spanish Succession. Obverse, Louis XIV of France; reverse, his grandson, Philip, Duke of Anjou, placed on the throne of Spain by Louis (see Appendix 1).
2 Portrait of Louis XIV.
3 The Treaty of Passarowitz 1718. On the reverse George I points to Morea on a globe, within a rich tent. The treaty was between the Germans, Turks and Venetians, with George I, King of England, Duke of Brunswick and Luneburg, Arch-Treasurer of the Holy Roman Empire and Elector of Hanover acting as mediator, the Turks having taken Morea from the Venetians. Struck in silver and bronze and engraved by John Croker (1670–1741), a prolific medallist during the whole of the period of the war. MI 2, 437/39.
4 Death of the Duke of Marlborough, 1722. Struck in silver and bronze by Dassier (1676–1763), another prolific medallist of the period. MI 2, 457/68.
5 Coronation of George II, 1727. An official coronation medal. Engraved by Croker and struck in gold, silver and bronze. The reverse shows the king seated in King Edward's chair, used for coronations (including that of the present Queen) since Edward II (1307–27). The chair is faithfully reproduced but the Stone of Scone is hidden behind the quatrefoil decorations below the seat. MI 2, 479/4.
6 Prince Frederick created Prince of Wales, 1729. Struck in bronze-gilt and bronze and engraved by Dassier. Frederick, who reached the age of twenty-one in 1728, was introduced to the Privy Council in December and created Prince of Wales in January 1729. A good example of allegorical representation, the obverse shows the Prince being invested with his coronet of rank by Fame (l) and Britannia (r). The reverse, an eagle training a young bird to fly from the summit of high mountains towards the sun, with ships and the sea in the background, alludes to the King introducing the Prince to the business of his life. Frederick died in 1751, before his father (1760), thus leaving the throne vacant for his own eldest son, who became George III. MI 2, 489/29.
7 Marriage of William, Prince of Orange, and Princess Anne, the Princess Royal, 1734, engraved by Martin Holtzhey (1697–1764) a Dutch medallist. Good miniature portraits, symbolic reverse. MI 2, 506/54. Very rare, several types.

PLATE VI

1 The Industrial Revolution. Matthew Boulton (1728–1809) one of its architects. Memorial medal by C. H. Kuchler, 1809.
2 Boulton's partner, James Watt (1736–1819), who made the steam engine a commercial proposition. Engraved by George Mills (1792–1824) commemorating Watt's death.
3 Struck at the world's first steam-powered mint at Soho and presented by Boulton to every man who took part at Trafalgar. Engraved by Kuchler, in gold for admirals, and in silver, silvered copper, gilt copper, copper and pewter. An edge inscription reads TO THE HEROES OF TRAFALGAR FROM M. BOULTON.
4 (a-c) The world's first underwater tunnel, apart from coalmine workings. Started by Sir M. I. Brunel in 1824 and finished by his son, I. K. Brunel, builder of the Great Western Railway in 1834. First opened as an underwater street between Wapping and Rotherhithe, now used by LT and BR trains. Reverse, the method devised by the engineer, after studying the *Teredo navalis* boring into ships' timbers. (b) and (c) entrances; some specimens show a horse and cart, though how it got there is not explained.
5 Meanwhile George Stephenson and his son Robert were building the Liverpool & Manchester Railway, opened 1830. The reverse full of detail, with disaster apparently imminent, as there is no embankment ahead of the locomotive.
6 Although it was *The Rocket,* now in the Science Museum, that brought the Stephensons' fame, they had already built other locomotives. This shows an early example, built by George, 1816. Signed J. S. and A. B. Wyon (1836–73 and 1837–84), thus probably contemporary. Dendy Marshall, who had a copper uniface impression taken before 'No. 2' was added, considers it to be the locomotive that was working at Springwell Colliery in 1863, and still working at Killingworth in 1879. If so it could be the fourth engine built by Stephenson, said by Young, (Timothy Hackworth) to have been built in 1816 and much altered before reaching its final state. The artists may have seen it at work when they designed their medal and been told it was built in 1816.
7 Portrait of the Duke of Wellington who, as Prime Minister, attended the opening of the Liverpool & Manchester Railway, though he had little sympathy for such new-fangled ideas. The general confusion in which the opening ceremony took place could hardly have altered his opinion. There are almost endless medals showing the Iron Duke.

PLATE VII

1 Thomas Telford and his spectacular work, the Menai suspension bridge, engraved by William Wyon and struck in 1837.

2 Two further views of the Liverpool & Manchester Railway. The obverse is fairly typical of artistic misrepresentation, not uncommon on medals dealing with mechanical subjects. The scene is Edgehill incline, the terminus for locomotives, the trains being lowered down the incline by cable, through a tunnel to the Liverpool station. The cables were worked by fixed steam engines, which also hauled the trains up the incline. The chimneys were hidden by the two towers, left and right, designed in the Moorish style with an arch between them. The detail of this structure is not as shown in some contemporary prints. The two tall chimneys in the background probably did not exist, and are wrongly placed if they are supposed to be those of the fixed engines. They appear to spring from the triple tunnels, the centre containing the main line, the other two leading to Crown Street Yard and to the railway's workshops respectively. On contemporary engravings neither tunnels nor chimneys can be seen. The walls were of stone, with staircases leading down to the railway from each side. The public did walk about the railway in the early days and trains could be seen travelling either way on either track. The reverse is similar to that already shown on Plate V, but is the much larger viaduct over the Sankey valley. The locomotive is probably *The Rocket*.

3 The Grand Junction Railway was authorised in 1833 and completed in 1837, connecting Liverpool and Manchester with Birmingham. It was the world's first trunk railway. The reverse shows Stephenson's fine viaduct over the Weaver, near Northwich.

4 Crystal Palace, as designed by Paxton and erected in Hyde Park for the Great Exhibition of 1851. Many medals were awarded to the exhibitors, most of them engraved by Wyon. The Palace was later moved to Sydenham, additions were made including two isolated towers, and it was used as an exhibition and cultural centre. It was destroyed by fire in 1936.

5 Seeing the Crystal Palace in the south, the residents of north London demanded a similar centre. Alexandra Palace was, therefore, erected on the heights of Muswell Hill. This medal probably shows the first Palace, burned down almost at its opening, as the towers of the second were slightly different. The Palace was the home of the world's first public television service.

6 See p 96 for reference to the history of the Louvre. This medal, one of three similar, shows some of the work of Perrault, 1667.

PLATE VIII

1 Mainly Coronations, Miniature of William IV (1830–37), the last occasion on which these tiny medals were struck. They were sometimes thrown to the crowd of spectators watching the coronation procession, and were struck in various metals, including gold.

2 Coronation of Queen Victoria (1837–1901), engraved by Pistrucci and struck at the Royal Mint. As in modern times the coronation takes place one year after the accession, the date shown is that of the coronation year. Struck in gold, silver and bronze.

3 The Corporation of the City of London usually entertains the new monarch to a banquet at Guildhall soon after the accession. Queen Victoria, who ascended the throne in June 1837, made a formal visit to the City in November. William Wyon was commissioned to design this piece for the occasion. It forms one of a series marking important City events. The portrait for the British Imperial penny (black) and twopenny postage stamps printed between 1840 and 1879 inclusive was drawn from the obverse of this medal. The reverse shows the entrance to Guildhall, still standing, though the hall itself suffered damage in World War II.

4 By way of comparison with medals 2 and 3, a poor unofficial portrait of Queen Victoria and the Prince Consort. A privately struck medal commemorating the launching by the Prince of Brunel's steamship *Great Britain* in 1843, the hull of which vessel has recently been returned to the Bristol dock from which it was launched, for the ship to be rebuilt.

5 Coronation of Edward VII (1901–10). Struck by the Royal Mint in two sizes and in gold, silver and bronze.

6 Coronation of George V (1910–36). Struck by the Royal Mint in the two sizes shown and in gold, silver and bronze.

7 Coronation of George VI (1936–52). Struck by the Royal Mint in two sizes—this is the smaller—and in gold, silver and bronze. These medals were supplied in fitted leather cases, sometimes to become a problem for the collector (see p 111).

8 There was no official coronation medal for Queen Elizabeth II, crowned 1953 (see p 88). Its place was taken by the cupro-nickel Coronation crown.

PLATE IX

1   The opening of Tower Bridge in 1894 by the Prince of Wales (later King Edward VII) on behalf of the now aged Queen Victoria. The royal steam yacht, *Victoria and Albert,* to serve for many more years till replaced by the Royal Yacht *Britannia,* passes downstream. The top of the Monument and the dome of St Paul's can be seen in the background. As the Port of London moves downstream, the bridge is about to become a museum piece. Its ornate towers are only a cladding for a metal structure, and were intended to harmonise with the Tower of London, seen dimly over the right-hand suspension cables.

2   Soon after the coronation of George V, his eldest son, Edward (later King Edward VIII and then Duke of Windsor), was invested as Prince of Wales at Carnarvon (sic) Castle. This official medal recalls the recent investiture of the present Prince. The mis-spelling of the name caused some comment.

3   One of the few British medals marking World War I (1914–18) —the naval battles of Heligoland Bight, 1914, and Dogger Bank, 1915. Struck by Spink & Son in gold, silver and bronze in 1916.

4   Privately struck commemorative medal of the bombardment of Scarborough in the early days of World War I. This and medal 3 above are good examples of an artist dividing his area in cantons to show several subjects on the same medal.

5   Unofficial piece commemorating the victory of the Allies in World War I. The medal has been pierced, and may have been worn, also unofficially.

6   Middlesex County Council medal commemorating the Silver Jubilee of King George V, 1935. Its octagonal shape is unusual but gives the artist a number of cantons on the obverse in which the legend and national emblems are placed. The reverse is not so happily designed, the artist having obviously had difficulty with the placing of the lettering in the lower legend.

PLATE X

1 An example of the series (see p 77), issued by the Art Union of London.

2 Lincoln Cathedral. There is a large series of medals of cathedrals and churches, many, as this one, by the Belgian medallist Jacques Wiener (1815–99), whose fine detailed work compares favourably with that of the Wyons.

3 The 200th anniversary of the British Museum's foundation, by the contemporary medallist Paul Vincz.

4 The Churchill memorial medal (see p 89) struck by Spink & Son.

PLATE XI

1 Obverse, commemorating William Penn, by the French sculptor and medallist Emile Rogat (1770–1850) struck in 1844.

2 Obverse, of similar type, commemorating Lord Tennyson, by the British sculptor J. W. Minton, who produced a series of portrait medals of distinguished Englishmen.

3 Obverse, portrait of Lord Baden-Powell (1857–1941), soldier and author, founder of the Boy Scout and Girl Guide movements. He was named Robert after his godfather Robert Stephenson, the engineer. Struck by Spink & Son in gold, silver and bronze.

4 Royal Geographical Society's medal, with portrait of Dr David Livingstone. Specially struck for presentation to members of Livingstone's last expedition, and to those who carried his body down to the coast after his death. Only sixty were struck.

5 The same Society's commemoration of Sir Vivian Fuchs' trans-Antarctic expedition, 1955–8. Presented to members of the expedition. Very rare.

6 The Sanford Saltus medal, presented in gold to members of the British Numismatic Society judged to have made an outstanding contribution to numismatic research, in the form of a Paper or Papers appearing in the Society's publication, the *British Numismatic Journal*. The award, which is made by ballot, was founded by John Sanford Saltus by a gift of £200 in 1910, and is made triennially. Only about twenty-one have been struck so far.

7 Henley Horticultural Society prize, a typical example of a privately struck award.

8 Olympic medal, awarded at the Games held in London in 1908, in gold, silver and bronze.

PLATE XII

1   Bronze, struck by Cunard to commemorate the commissioning in 1936 of the greatest of all liners, the RMS *Queen Mary*. It was presented gratis by the Company.

2   Bronze, struck by the London, Midland & Scottish Railway in 1938 to commemorate the centenary of its ancestor, The London & Birmingham, opened in 1838. The obverse shows the Doric Arch with two of its flanking lodges, designed by Philip Hardwick as the grand entrance to the original London terminus of the railway at Euston.

3   Struck in 1903 to commemorate the 500th anniversary of the Battle of Shrewsbury, 1403, which was fought between Henry IV (1399–1413) and insurgents led by Henry Percy, whose object was to join his forces with those of Owen Glendower. The minor legend on the obverse, REG APPLIED FOR, is unusual, and is an attempt to 'copyright' the medal.

PLATE XIII

1 Struck to commemorate the 400th anniversary of the discovery of America, this US medal has a reverse which completely describes its purpose.

2 Modern medallic portrait of Tolstoy.

3 Not so self-explanatory as the earlier medals illustrating railways, this modern piece marks the electrification of the Paris–Rouen–Le Havre route in 1967.

These three pieces are reasonably typical of modern medallic art and of medals issued by medal clubs and societies of the type mentioned in the text (p 95).

PLATE XIV

1 Two further modern medals. Louis XIV, the Sun King, and his magnificent Palace of Versailles, seen on the reverse in plan, with part of the gardens.
2 A final warning?

A purpose-built medal collection cabinet.

PLATE XVI

Medals displayed in a glass-topped showcase.

THE MEDAL AS AN ART FORM
— ITS HISTORY

CHAPTER I

THE MEDAL AS AN ART FORM — ITS HISTORY

AS FAR as we know the ancient Greek civilisation, which evolved the coin in the very late seventh century BC, did not take the next step, obvious to us now, and strike in metal an object solely designed to commemorate some person or some event of historic importance.

The coins of the ancient Greeks in part commemorated their gods and goddesses, as well as the many city-states of which their empire was composed. But their purpose in this respect was to show from which city-state the coins came, rather than directly to commemorate either the city, the god or the goddess. The coin only tried to show what such places and personages should look like. In the event such coins 'commemorated' the city and its divinity, but the pieces were coins, not medals.

The striking of the metals electrum, gold and silver, into money was taken as far as the strength of the metals used to make the dies would then allow. This is illustrated by coins the size of the decadrachms of Syracuse, struck c.410 BC. These magnificent pieces are about $1\frac{1}{4}$ inches in diameter though they are not completely circular. By the fifth century BC the Graeco-Scythians had also made bronze pieces at Olbia which were about $2\frac{5}{8}$ inches in diameter, but they were cast in a mould, not struck between two dies.

Eucratides, a Greek general and later king, caused the largest ancient gold coin in existence to be struck when he produced a piece of the value of 20 Attic staters, weighing 168.05 grammes, and a fraction over 2 inches at its greatest diameter. This piece was definitely commemorative since it marked the triumph of Eucratides over Demetrius, against whom he had revolted c.175 BC, wresting Bactria from him and finally driving him into the eastern Punjab while annexing the country of the Indus to Bactria. Eucratides was the first Greek king to describe himself as 'the Great' on a coin. In reference to this large piece Macdonald states that 'No other king or city of ancient times was ever responsible for so ostentatious a display of opulence'. Large was the piece indeed, but though commemorating a triumph it was still a coin.

In past times it was usual to describe certain large Greek coins, such as that of Eucratides, as medallions, particularly since many of them were in various ways commemorative. The medallic concept, however, is not appropriate as a description of Greek coins and Seltman consigns such a concept firmly to the wastepaper basket. Similarly it was once popular to describe certain large 'brass' pieces struck by the Romans as medals. Smyth, in his catalogue of Roman Imperial *Large Brass Medals*, 1884, sustained this ancient idea, but this is equally wrong and has long since been discarded by scholars. On such an analogy one might well be tempted to describe as medals many of the Roman pieces which were larger than those usually accepted as coins: for instance the clumsy cast aes grave, the as (Liberal standard) post 235 BC, the semis or the dupondius.

Even so the Romans made great use of the coin as a commemorative piece, giving it in many cases a political or propaganda twist. People, events and buildings are all commemorated on their coins. But perhaps it should be pointed out here that any coin with the head of a ruler by way of device may, from some points of view, be said to commemorate that person, though this is not the basic purpose for which the piece was struck.

With so much of local importance being commemorated on coins, and with larger than normal coins being produced, either by casting or striking, the Romans were gradually moving towards the pure medallion or medal. A number of monetiform pieces, not strictly coins, began to appear. Of such were the 'medallions' or aes, used for distribution on special occasions and not struck to any fixed standard of size or weight. Other pieces of gold and silver are also frequently referred to as medallions, though they are normally multiples of the aureus and the denarius in the same way as the present British 50p is a multiple of the 1p.

Certainly there were bronze medallions of the second century, AD commemorative pieces not destined for use as currency. Of such are the series of the Emperor Antoninus Pius, in preparation for the games celebrating the 900th year of Rome. These pieces illustrated the early history of the city showing such subjects as the landing of Aeneas, and the story of Hercules and Cacus. In the later Imperial series, following AD 295 and the reform of Diocletian, there were medallions in gold, silver and bronze. There are also pieces, known as 'Contorniates', made of base metal with turned-up edges, though these were probably playing-counters used in some form of game.

The medallion or medal was certainly struck by the Romans and thus, as an art form, became established. Of all the Roman medallions which have come down to us, certainly one of the finest was discovered in a hoard at Arras in comparatively recent times. It commemorated the recovery of Britain by Constantius I Chlorus (AD 305) and his entry into London. The largest piece in the hoard, some of which was melted down—the worst piece of vandalism in numismatic history—showed Constantius riding up to the gate of London while a suppliant woman, 'Lon-(dinium') kneels before him. On the river Thames are soldiers in a galley, while the gate seen beyond the woman looks not unlike part of the 'White Tower' to be built centuries later. This fine piece is about $1\frac{5}{8}$ inches in diameter and is definitely a commemorative medal, though some scholars hold that this piece might have been used as money in some form.

It will be seen, therefore, that medals are usually larger than coins, though there is no hard and fast rule on this point and we shall certainly come across some which are smaller than coins. This larger size would probably in part be intended to prevent medals from being mistaken for coins. Such a mistake is still not uncommon today. The larger size may well have been brought into being by the artist, using the opportunity of the greater scope offered him to demonstrate his powers.

Another fundamental difference between the coin and the medal—a difference that should at once be made clear—is that of weight. Coins, being in a large measure derived from weights, are tied in tightly with a weight-scale. In the days when a coin had to contain as much silver or gold as it was worth—its intrinsic value—the very strictest limits of tolerance, bearing in mind the standard of accuracy of the weighing machines of the time, were laid down. Badly worn coins which had thus lost their full value were, eventually, taken out of circulation and melted down as a source of metal for new coins. Such a custom continued in Britain into the era of the gold sovereign and half sovereign, 1817 *et seq,* for as long as these coins were in general circulation. We read in the Annual Report of the Deputy Master and Comptroller of the Royal Mint frequent references to the withdrawal of numbers of worn sovereigns.

Even in our own times, when our British coins have no intrinsic value, their weight is still of great importance if only to achieve uniformity, regularise the cost of production, deter the forger, and enable the coins to operate the increasing number of automatic machines. With coins made of precious metal the fineness—the amount of alloy allowed to be added to the metal —was also of the highest importance. Debased coins, posing as of a fineness they did not possess, were soon discounted in international trade and could spell ruin, as Henry VIII was soon to find.

The commemorative medal is restricted to none of these considerations of size, weight and fineness. It can be of any size, of any weight and of any metal. Its main resemblance to the true coin is that it is a flan of metal—though other substances have been used—is usually circular but, as with some coins, not always so, and made in the same way—by placing this flan of metal between two previously engraved dies, which are struck either with a hammer or by mechanical means. As with some coins, medals can also be cast. In recent times they have even come to be 'cast' in man made plastic materials; but here the resemblance between the two art forms ends.

Returning to the history of the medal, with the invasion of the Roman Empire by the Goths, Visigoths, Ostrogoths and Vandals, the art of striking money and medals of high artistic standard became lost. The cycle of experiment and discovery had practically to begin all over again. Such pieces as the gold medallion of Theodoric the Ostrogoth are known, but in the main we see little more of the medal till its revival during the Renaissance.

By this period civilisation had pulled itself painfully through the ages of war, pillage and conquest, through the darkness of continuous turmoil, and was once more getting back into the sunlight of comparative order and limited progress. In this new atmosphere art became valued once more and artists, often under patronage in various forms, began to flourish.

Such patronage has continued to be given almost unbroken till our own times. Thus we now get bodies like the Church of England commissioning Coventry Cathedral—the work of many artists—industry inviting art to embellish its buildings with statues and portraits for its board rooms, and organisations like the British Academy and the Arts Council devoting themselves to the patronage of the arts on a wide scale—arts which might otherwise die from lack of support.

With the great Renaissance revival in art and learning the medal began to reappear as an art form. It first made its reappearance in the courts of the ambitious and splendour-loving princes of North Italy, where it was seen as a means of self-glorification and commemoration both of the princes and of people of importance.

To Antonio di Puccio Pisano, usually called Pisanello (c.1380–

1451), scholars attribute the creation of the Renaissance medal. Widely known as a painter, and probably the most renowned portrait painter of his time, it was within the last decade of his life that he added still further to his reputation by medallic creations. It is generally accepted that Pisanello was inspired to take up medallic art by the study of Flemish-Burgundian medallions, the cast gold medals made for the duc de Berry, and by the Byzantine gold medal of Constantine, to which the artist's earliest medal bore many similarities. This was his medal of John VIII Paleologos, Emperor of Constantinople (1425–48) who came to Ferrara in 1438 in an attempt to obtain from the Council, there assembled, aid against the Turks.

It was soon found that the prevailing state of metallurgical knowledge restricted the size of medals. Large dies, engraved in high relief, soon broke up under the stresses of striking. Equally, large flans of metal cracked and many similar problems arose. Thus we find among the many fine medals of the Italian Renaissance, which was leading the world in art at this time, many cast pieces. Not a few of these have a plain, flat reverse, without any design.

When removed from the mould the cast medal was skilfully worked upon with graving tools to give it a clean, high finish. Such medals when cast in bronze frequently have a granular appearance in the plain areas. Gold and silver pieces may have a streaked look, where the graving tool has worked.

During the period under review, the fifteenth and sixteenth centuries, da Vinci, Cellini and many other great artists and thinkers were working on the various problems posed by striking metal with large dies. By the end of the period some of the problems had been partly solved, or at least a greater measure of success in production could be expected. These pioneers had, in fact, evolved a method of striking blanks or flans of metal into coins and medals.

The struck medal was produced by placing a prepared flan of metal between two dies which were placed in a screw press. In such a press one die was fitted to the bedplate and the other was attached to the lower end of a screw shaft. This shaft had a heavily weighted capstan or wheel on the top. By spinning the screw shaft downwards with as much manpower as was available —ultimately two or four men—the upper die was made to descend sharply. At the end of its descent the upper die struck a heavy blow on the flan of metal which, held in place on the lower die by a rim or a collar, could not move. The lower die thus created an upward pressure on the flan, the metal of which 'flowed' into the designs cut into the upper and lower dies.

Improved in various ways over the centuries this type of screw press remained in use until manpower was replaced by steam power. Since then, though the coin press developed to produce a 'squeezing' pressure, the medal press still in many cases depends on heavy impact, more than one blow usually being necessary to produce a medal from the thick metal flan.

Metallurgical difficulties remained for a considerable time, particularly in the striking of pure copper, as opposed to bronze, which was still to present problems as late as the eighteenth century, as Sir Isaac Newton was to find. In spite of all the difficulties and limitations, by the middle of the sixteenth century medallic art was spreading throughout Europe, including Britain. Some of the earliest medals to appear in this country did so in or about the reign of Henry VIII (1509–47). We can, therefore, now take a look at some aspects of their production in Britain.

THE MEDAL IN BRITAIN — SIXTEENTH TO EIGHTEENTH CENTURIES

CHAPTER 2

THE MEDAL IN BRITAIN — SIXTEENTH TO EIGHTEENTH CENTURIES

THE MEDAL began to be appreciated in Britain during the reign of Henry VIII (1509–47), a robust and colourful monarch who might well have enjoyed many of the twentieth-century portraits of himself that have been presented on film and television. In dealing with the medals of this period it must be borne in mind that many of them were struck in Europe, in the Low Countries in particular, and that the British medallists were feeling their way in what was to them a new art form.

The British Museum Catalogue (*Medallic Illustrations of the History of Great Britain and Ireland to the death of George II*, hereafter referred to as BMC) of its large collection lists some medals struck by such commercial medallists as Dassier, who commemorated many persons of importance long after their death. Jean Dassier was, in fact, 'one of the best of the eighteenth century Medallists'. Then as now there was a market for medals recording some of the persons and events of the past.

A parallel may be drawn with the many medals now being struck to commemorate such famous people as William Shakespeare by organisations devoted to his works and to his memory. Such medals, struck long after the event, attempt to recreate the past and show to the present, persons and events which are still the subject of interest and study. Such medals usually have a commercial background and more will be said on this point later.

All this being understood, the reader can now look at some of the medals commemorating past events in Britain with a wider

THE MEDAL IN BRITAIN—SIXTEENTH TO EIGHTEENTH CENTURIES

appreciation. They are not necessarily contemporary works of art; they may be contemporary but have been struck abroad; but they record the scene as it was passing or appears to have been passing at that time. The medal, unbounded by time, can look back into the past through the eyes of historians and medallic artists of the present. It may thus glamorise the past when it is struck many years after the event which it records.

This freedom to range over the centuries gives the medallic artist scope not enjoyed by the designers of coins. These must be struck during their own period of history, though commemorative coins can portray some past person or event. The Kennedy half dollar and the Lincoln cent are examples but such issues are few when set against the millions of coins struck daily.

The medal collector can thus take into his cabinet quite recently struck medals, which reflect some past event that comes within his collecting theme. While he must bear in mind that they were struck long after the event, he can still appreciate them as a quasi-record of past history. To make such a statement may offend the purist, the artist and the historian. The medal in Britain is going through a renaissance and the student and the collector are, happily, on the increase. The whole situation will sort itself out in time. Inferior medals will eventually be discarded, after they have been duly recorded; and the winnowing hand of time and experience will eventually sort out that which is good, worthy of collecting and of reasonable interest.

Let us now return to the development of the medal over about 100 years, between the reigns of Henry VIII (1509–47) and Charles I (1625–49). During this period many medals of British interest were being struck either at home or abroad.

During the reign of Henry VIII there were quite a large number of portrait medals. A small series concerned John Colet, founder of St. Paul's School: its erection started in 1509 while its endowment was carried out in 1512. Two further medals, neither contemporary, record the death of James IV of Scotland in 1513. The first was once thought to have been designed during the king's preparation for his fatal invasion of England but is now considered to be of later sixteenth century Continental workmanship. Richard Fox, founder of Corpus Christi College, Oxford, in 1516, is also recorded; as are Sir Thomas More, d. 1535, whose medal is thought to be of the seventeenth or eighteenth century; Myles Coverdale, translator of the Bible; Michael Mercator, the geographer, 1539; Thomas Cromwell, beheaded in 1540; and many more. Not a few of the people medallically recorded were concerned in Henry's matrimonial turmoils.

On a sterner note is the medal of Pope Paul III recording the excommunication of Henry in 1538—the king who, for his earlier writings, had been granted the title of 'Defender of the Faith'. This medal, probably by Valerio Belli, is in high relief and cast. Rising above Papal authority, Henry is recorded as head of his reformed church in 1545; and in the same year as supreme head of the church.

The accent of the medallist during this reign was mainly on portraiture and a most valuable record is thus handed down to the student and collector.

In the next reign, that of Henry's only son, Edward VI (1547–53), innocent part cause of his father's matrimonial tangles, the coronation of the child is marked by a series of medals. Here started a custom, not carried on as a continuity till the reign of James I (1607–25) *et seq*, of striking a medal to mark the coronation of our monarchs. The custom was discontinued after the reign of George VI (1936–52) when it was broken in favour of the commemorative crown piece of 1953. Collecting coronation medals is a theme in which more than a few collectors have specialised.

The reign of Edward VI was short, but there was time to record the cession of Boulogne—precursor to the loss of our last European possession, Calais, in the next reign—the founding of Birmingham Free Grammar School, 1552, and of Christ's Hospital in 1553. Dassier, the more or less faithful recorder of events

THE MEDAL IN BRITAIN—SIXTEENTH TO EIGHTEENTH CENTURIES

long after, adds a couple of 'portrait' medals to those of the reign.

During the troubled reign of Mary (1553–4), Henry's daughter who now succeeded, and of Philip and Mary (1554–8) after her ill-starred marriage to the Spanish Prince, there was much to record. Lady Jane Grey (1553), the 'pretender' to the throne, figures at once, as does Mary Queen of Scots (1553). Her turbulent life and later tragic execution were to span this and part of the next reign (Elizabeth I), though the early events in her colourful career took place in the then far-away Scotland.

There are portrait medals of both Mary and Philip, and the Restoration of Popery (1554–5) and the burning of the Protestant martyrs Ridley, Latimer and Cranmer at Smithfield are also recorded. The Siege of St. Quentin, 1557, and the loss of Calais, 1558, are also depicted on medals, and the faithful Dassier adds a few later 'portraits' to the series. Two possibly military rewards were issued, but their off shoots—the 'war medal' and 'decoration'—were not yet in being.

By the reign of Elizabeth I (1558–1603) the medal as an art form and as a means of recording contemporary history had established itself. The BMC lists 195 pieces, some of which were catalogued as counters, seemingly used in place of money in games of chance, or by the exchequer for counting purposes on the chequer board—but this is a numismatic study outside our brief.

Elizabeth's accession (1558) was recorded by three pieces, all now rare. Mary, Queen of Scots, one of Elizabeth's 'political problems', appears on the scene at once, since in 1558 she married the Dauphin of France, who received the title of King of Scots. On the face of it this might not appear a matter of world-shaking importance, since Scotland was still a separate kingdom: but its implications were wider than might be supposed. By this marriage Mary became Queen of France on the death of Henry II and was also declared Queen of England by the French and Spanish courts. Her husband was now Francis II of France. If

Mary had any sons one of them might become King of France —with what implications for the kingdoms of England and Scotland?

On the other side of the medal, almost literally, was the implication that Francis II of France could be King of Scotland, and this fact was recorded by two, now rare, counters. However Francis II died in 1560, without issue, and Mary returned to Scotland, finally to die under the axe at Fotheringay Castle. This tragic event took place in 1587 and was not medallically recorded at that time. A single medal does exist, but it was of later striking, by Tassie, another eighteenth/nineteenth century medallic recorder of past events.

Elizabeth's reign was full of events that were worthy of medallic record. In the popular mind the crest of the historic wave came with the defeat of the Spanish Armada in 1588. Through the eyes of such patriotic writers as Charles Kingsley this great naval battle has tended to become over-played. A more sobering account, given in the *Dictionary of English History* is worth quoting in full if only to show how the medal, as a vehicle of propaganda, could be made to tell that part of the story selected for home consumption. The *Dictionary's* account is as follows:—

> The English Lord High Admiral, Lord Howard of Effingham, had thirty ships of the Royal Navy, and a large number of volunteer ships, with him [cf evacuation of Dunkirk in World War II] and was assisted by Drake, Hawkins, Frobisher, Winter, Raleigh, and other seamen. The Armada steered for Calais Road. On Sunday, July 31, some fighting took place, in which the unwieldy Spanish ships were completely out-manoeuvred. They were built so extremely high, and drew so few feet of water in proportion, that they could not carry enough sail. The handy English vessels closed and drew off as they pleased. Our seamen, acting on the principle which has always been followed in the English navy, trusted to their rapid and accurate artillery fire, and refused all temptations to board the enemy, whose vessels were crowded with soldiers.

THE MEDAL IN BRITAIN—SIXTEENTH TO EIGHTEENTH CENTURIES

The account continues:—

> On Tuesday, August 9, the Armada, greatly diminished by loss of vessels, which had been sunk or compelled to strike, or driven on shore, was drifting helplessly on the coast of Zeeland. A sudden change of wind saved it for the moment, but the crews had no more stomach for the fight. By the next day they had quite lost heart and began to fly to the north.

The account then states that there was no effectual pursuit, since Elizabeth's ships had been ill provisioned with powder, shot and food, and had put to sea in a hurry. Drake, it is popularly said, refused to put to sea till he had finished his game of bowls, while the *Dictionary* states that:—

> The brunt of the fighting fell on the vessels of the Royal Navy; the volunteers, though they proved the spirit of the nation and helped to make a moral impression on the Spaniards, did comparatively little of the real work.

Against the above factual account a number of medals which record the defeat of the Spanish Armada carry such legends as 'He blew and they were scattered', 'the Spanish fleet came, went, was', and 'the Spaniards flee and perish, no one pursuing'. In fact the victory was poised on a knife-edge, as so many victories have been.

The most important medal of the Elizabethan series is considered to be that called 'Dangers Averted', struck in 1589. The obverse has a fine portrait bust of the queen full face, regally crowned and dressed. The Latin legend translates 'no other circle in the whole world more rich' and alludes to the queen's crown being as fully established in power and real wealth as any in Europe. The reverse shows a bay tree, uninjured by lightning and winds, flourishing on an island, with a legend that translates 'not even dangers affect it'. In the distance beyond the island are two ships. Of the two main varieties, one has ER in the field of the reverse of the medal. Not only is this a particularly fine cast and chased medal but, though it is unsigned, it is now regarded as the work of Nicholas Hilliard (1547–1619), goldsmith and jeweller to Elizabeth and a famous miniature painter.

The medal came at a time when there must have been considerable satisfaction in England. As pointed out in BMC (vol. I 154, nos 129–33), it was possibly a naval award,—'when the greatest dangers to Elizabeth had ceased. The Queen of Scots was dead and the plots of which she had been the cause were at an end; James had been conciliated; the Armada defeated; the Duke of Guise was dead; France and the Vatican were baffled'. The bay tree alludes to the legend that it was incapable of injury from lightning and also preserved the place where it grew or the people who wore it.

Among the remainder of the many more medals commemorating important events in this colourful reign are a number of portrait pieces of the queen and others of importance, with the inevitable Dassier medal bringing up the rear.

Although war medals, decorations and orders, as we now know them, are outside the scope of this work, a word must be said here about them, since we are now coming to the point in history at which they were probably established.

It had long been the habit for medals, especially those given by the sovereign, to be worn, frequently on a chain round the neck as a form of adornment—costume jewellery we should now call it—while at the same time marking the distinction that had been conferred on the wearer by the gift. There was, however, no set pattern of awards at this time, the early Stuart period, nor for several centuries to come, except for the Most Noble Order of the Garter, founded circa 1348, the Most Honourable Order of the Bath, originally founded 1399, and Baronet's Badges, instituted in 1629.

In the reign of Charles I (1625–49) a number of badges, usually oval, of silver or silver gilt, made of thin embossed plates united by a broad substantial rim, began to make their appearance. Some have come to be known as royalist badges, and it is considered that they were frequently worn by the king's supporters. Others showed commanders, such as the Earl of Manchester. All had a loop for suspension on a ribbon or chain.

In 1642 (the Battle of Edgehill), at least two such badges are catalogued as military awards. In 1643 Charles I, by special warrant addressed to Sir William Parkhurst and Thomas Bushell, Wardens of the Mint which had been set up by the king at Oxford, commanded a badge which is known as the 'Forlorn Hope' military award. It was to be worn 'on the breast of every man who shall be certified under the hands of their Commanders-in-Chief to have done us faithful service in the forlorn hope'. It is considered very doubtful if the medal was ever so awarded and worn.

Rewards and awards were also issued by Cromwell, again mostly with rings for suspension. He commissioned one military award while he was in Scotland, after the Battle of Dunbar, the artist Thomas Simon travelling north to make his portrait for the obverse. The battle took place on 3 September 1650 and on 7 September the Commons resolved 'that their special thanks be conveyed to the Lord-General for his eminent services at the great victory of Dunbar, and that His Excellency be desired to return their thanks also to the officers and soldiers of the army, and that a number of gold and silver medals be distributed among them'. The design of the medal was suggested by Cromwell himself.

In the absence of proof that the 'Forlorn Hope' medal was ever awarded, many collectors and students consider the Dunbar Medal the first official military award for services in the field. From Cromwell's time until the early nineteenth century, when the present pattern of military medals was established many military and naval awards and rewards not intended for wearing were issued and these are usually to be found in the cabinets of the collectors of commemorative medals.

Throughout the Commonwealth and the reigns of Charles II,

THE MEDAL IN BRITAIN—SIXTEENTH TO EIGHTEENTH CENTURIES

James II, William and Mary, and William III, covering the period 1649 to 1702, the majority of the large number of medals struck were in silver, with silver gilt and gold appearing from time to time. Such metals as lead were occasionally used. Towards the end of the period medals in copper or bronze, usually described by the abbreviation AE, began to appear in increasing numbers. Some of the finest bronze medals, both artistically and technically, were struck in the reign of Anne (1702–14).

It should be mentioned that during the reign of William and Mary (1688–94), most of the medals were issued in Holland, as might be expected, since William was Prince of Orange. During the joint monarchy foreign production of medals for England probably reached its peak. Bearing in mind that Europe was usually a step or two ahead of England in the techniques of making coins and medals, some very fine examples of the latter could be expected and were produced. Artists such as Jan Smeltzing of Nimeguen were leading the field in the Low Countries, and Heinrich Muller of Nuremburg, Jan Luder, and in Britain, George Bower, were prominent medallists. The collector and student should study the BMC and assess all the interest and implications of the medal design scene of the period.

With the War of the Spanish Succession starting immediately on the accession of Queen Anne there was soon much to commemorate. Moreover the medal was now increasingly used as a vehicle of propaganda, all the famous battles and sieges, in what seems an endless list, being faithfully commemorated by artists of considerable distinction. (See Appendix 1.)

The extent to which the medals of this reign are still available, often in considerable numbers, underlines the wholesale manner in which they were pressed into propaganda service. It is, of course, highly likely that this was in direct imitation of the Louis XIV series being issued in France. (See also Appendix 1.)

Though silver was still being extensively used for these medals, with gold making an occasional appearance, the baser metals, copper and bronze, now became firmly established. Many of the medals struck in these metals have a most pleasing tone. Until the death of George II in 1760 they are all carefully catalogued in the BMC which is the Bible of the collector and student of the medals of this period. Most of the medals themselves can be seen in the British Museum.

We have already mentioned Dassier, whose work was good, often of a very high standard. His series of famous Englishmen, 1739 and later, is considered as possibly his finest work, particularly the medal of Alexander Pope.

THE INDUSTRIAL REVOLUTION AND THE MEDAL

CHAPTER 3

THE INDUSTRIAL REVOLUTION AND THE MEDAL

WE ARE now about to see the medal go through a considerable proliferation, brought about in part by the Industrial Revolution.

It should be made clear at this point that no one is permitted to strike a flan of metal in such a way that it is, or could be, taken for a coin, and that this rule does not apply to the commemorative medal so long as it does not look like money. The medal is therefore allowed complete freedom of production within this limit. In view of what is about to happen to it, it is worth pausing for a moment and reducing this general statement to a particular instance.

Anyone who is prepared to meet the cost of production can have a commemorative medal struck. If you feel that the birth of your first child, your silver wedding, or your accomplishment of some event of importance is worth the cost of striking a medal, you can go ahead and commission such a medal.

The cost of your medal will vary according to the artist you employ to design it, the firm you employ to strike it and the metal in which you have it struck.

Of artists there are many but, subject to the technical limitations of striking any particular design, you could well design the medal yourself. Only if you produce a design that will not translate into metal will it be turned down by the firm asked to strike it.

There are also many private firms that have minting machinery and can strike your medal. Spink & Son, the Royal Medallists, have the necessary equipment and will discuss the whole matter with you before you embark on such an idea. So will the Royal Mint itself. Both would be prepared to accept your contract. Both would provide you with the services of an artist skilled in coin and medal design, who would submit a scheme or, alternatively, tell you what is wrong with your own conception and show you how it could be adapted to the metal medium.

The choice of metal is simply a matter of cost, as are the other two. You can have your medal in platinum or gold if you can afford it, or in silver, bronze, pewter, lead, brass or tin. You can have any of the latter metals overlaid with gilt and made to look like, but not to last as long as, gold itself.

These facts being established, the next point to be considered is the impact of this freedom of action and of the Industrial Revolution on the medal.

The Industrial Revolution turned on two power packs—coal and steam. Coal as a means of obtaining warmth had been in use in Britain since the reign of Elizabeth I. That it was a power pack was not brought to fruition till James Watt improved the already existing steam engine, originally developed into a reasonably practical appliance by Newcomen (1663–1729). Watt, with the help of Matthew Boulton, applied it, amongst other purposes, to the minting of money and the striking of medals. While Watt improved the engine, Boulton improved minting machinery. Together this team went into action at Boulton's private mint at Soho in Birmingham. This application of steam power to minting was apparently minor though, in the long run, it was to affect the money in our pockets today.

Faced with no restrictions on medal striking and with steam power and improved minting machinery, the medal industry of the eighteenth and nineteenth centuries—a small one but an industry nonetheless—rose to the occasion. With no picture postcards, no films, no radio or television, the medal proliferated.

There was much to commemorate. McAdam was building roads, Telford constructing bridges and canals, Stephenson, Brunel and many others laying out railways—these latter themselves powered by a mobile steam appliance known as the locomotive. There were Nelson and Wellington bringing the war against France and Napoleon to a successful conclusion. There was the war against the American Colonies; the colourful and extravagant Prince Regent—later George IV; the reign of William IV (1830–37); the accession of the young Queen Victoria (1837–1901), her Jubilee in 1887; and many thousands of political, social, national and local events which could be, and were, commemorated by medals in practically all the metals mentioned above.

It is reasonable comment to say that the commercial commemorative medal of the eighteenth and nineteenth centuries stemmed in large part from Boulton's private mint at Soho. There were two sides to the activities of this mint. Boulton's campaigning for a copper coinage resulted in a contract, the first fruits of which were the 'Cartwheel' twopence and penny, showing that the coinage side of activities was definitely a commercial venture.

The other side of the Soho activities was the striking of commemorative medals. These were usually speculations, as are most of the commemorative medals issued since that time. Boulton's medals were of high artistic and technical standard. He employed some of the finest engravers of the period, such as C. H. Kuchler, and some of the finest artists to prepare drawings, portraits and sketches from which the engravers could work.

The important part played by Boulton in the history of the medal and in particular the contribution made by Kuchler, were the subject of extensive research by J. G. Pollard, which distilled into a Paper read before the Royal Numismatic Society and published in the 'Numismatic Chronicle' in 1970 (p 259 ff). Too long to analyse here, it deals exhaustively with some thirty four medals, and the costs involved; and gives extensive quotations from correspondence and a great deal of the history of one side of the Boulton family's activities.

Boulton and his Soho mint had a secondary effect on the commemorative medal. The Royal Mint, when it finally moved from the Tower of London between 1809 and 1812, was completely reformed and equipped with steam-powered minting machinery by Boulton and Watt. With the new plant came four artificers and a boy, engaged on permanent maintenance. Also transferred from Birmingham in 1811 were the Thomas Wyons, father and son, who with their collaterals and descendants were to sustain the engraving side of the Mint for some eighty years. The engravers employed by the Royal Mint at this time were allowed to work on private commissions, some of which, if medals, would be struck as contract work by the Mint machinery. Thus the medals from the Mint now measured up to Boulton's standards, achieving the high reputation for this class of work which the Mint maintains today.

Boulton and the Royal Mint were not alone in the striking of medals. Many new suppliers appeared and the output of medals increased in the way already indicated, which led in some cases to a lowering of art standards. Many of the nineteenth-century medals the collector will encounter are of the lowest form of speculative over-commercialised numismatic art. They cannot however be entirely neglected by the collector, since they make their contribution to the medallic record of history.

There was, nevertheless, always a good hard core of fine medallic work which carried the medal through the period till the flood diminished, leaving the medal to regain its high reputation as a slightly exclusive art form. This it maintained till a second wave of over-commercialism occurred in the second half of the twentieth century: but again, as will be seen later, some fine work remained.

Examples of the finest work of the nineteenth-century medallists came from such artists as Pistrucci (when he could be persuaded to produce anything), and in particular from the talented and industrious Wyon family, at least sixteen members of which were engaged in medal, coin, seal and die engraving over the period. The whole family is dealt with at length by Forrer in his *Biographical Dictionary of Medallists,* volume VI (1916), p 571 ff, which lists the large number of medals the Wyons produced. Indeed Wyon medals are an excellent collecting theme, offering the collector plenty of scope in work of high standard.

The great interest in medals at this time brought forth a series issued by James Mudie. These were styled 'National Medals' and commemorated the British victories over the French during the reign of George III, and were dedicated to George IV. The series contained some forty medals, struck either in bronze, silver or gold, though the writer has never seen a set in the latter metal. They were supplied in a book-form case containing velvet-lined trays in which the medals were placed. Because of the total weight of the whole set few such cases remain intact today. A descriptive book, detailing the history behind each medal, was included. It also contained a list of subscribers to the project, a further instance of commercial speculation. The whole was in imitation of a similar set produced by the French to mark the martial activities of Napoleon. Though both series have their rarities, in the main they are not rare, the two sets together forming a commentary on the opposite sides in the Napoleonic Wars.

Another fine series of medals was commissioned by the Corporation of the City of London, marking events of importance within the city. Many of these show some of the finest work of the Wyons. The first in the series, marking the visit of Queen Victoria to the Guildhall in 1837, is of more than usual interest. The portrait of the Queen was used for the British Imperial penny and twopenny postage stamps printed between 1840 and 1879, Henry Corbould drawing his portrait from William Wyon's design. Two other medals in the series, both by Wyon, are remarkable for their immense detail. One shows the Council Chamber at Guildhall and the other the interior of the Coal Exchange, the latter building only recently demolished.

To encourage interest in the medal and to attempt to keep medallic art at a high standard the Art Union of London was founded in 1837, the coronation year of Queen Victoria. The history, purpose and results in the field of art of this Union have been for many years obscure. Research carried out by G. K. Beaulah resulted in a Paper in the *British Numismatic Journal,* the organ of the British Numismatic Society, the Paper being published in 1967 (volume XXXVI, 1968, 179 ff). The following observations are based on this Paper.

The primary idea of the Union was that of encouraging interest in the fine arts and in particular to encourage British artists and manufacturers whose products, it was thought, were inferior to those in the same field which were being produced on the Continent. In return for an annual subscription of one guinea, members received each year a large engraving, the mass-production of which had become possible by a new electroplating process. This inexpensive method of production gave the Council of the Union a considerable cash surplus. This they dispersed on the purchase of original paintings from London exhibitions and on the manufacture for the Union of such objects as statuettes, vases and plaques, and on the production of medals.

In 1842 the Union embarked upon the production of 'the medallic series of the History of British Art' with the idea of fostering interest in the art of the medallist and of encouraging British die-engravers. In view of the flood of inferior medals during the nineteenth century, this idea would appear to have been laudable enough. About thirty medals in silver were struck each year. These were allocated to winners not qualifying for the more valuable prizes—presumably the statuettes, vases and plaques. The medals would thus appear as a kind of consolation prize, an attitude hardly in keeping with the purpose stated for their production.

Medals were also struck in bronze. These were available to any subscribers who might prefer them to the annual engraving —again a kind of consolation prize or second choice, hardly compatible with the stated purpose of the Union in respect of medallic art. In fact the Annual Report of the Union showed that relatively few people preferred the bronze medal to the engraving. Stock, therefore, it would appear, remained on hand and was eventually offered for sale to any member of the Union. By 1876 there were some 20,000 members and, though few are thought to have applied, some hundreds of bronze medals were dispersed—apparently a rather small percentage.

It is postulated that the silver medals were strictly controlled and that their distribution was confined to the thirty annual prizewinners mentioned above as not qualifying for the more valuable prizes. These were allocated by a draw or lottery. The Union was apparently of the opinion in 1842 that native medal engravers were a dying race, owing to lack of work. So far as the two famous Royal Mint engravers, William and Leonard Charles Wyon, were concerned, the reverse appears to have been the case. William Wyon was so busy that he took four years to deliver the Union's first medal. The Wyon family as a whole had never heard the word procrastination and were extremely hard working men.

It is worth noting that none of the Union medals was engraved by Pistrucci (1784–1855) for whom the position of Chief Medallist had been created at the Royal Mint. As a foreigner— he was an Italian—his appointment by William Wellesley Pole as an engraver of the reformed coinage of 1816 *et seq* had called forth much adverse comment in view of the work of the Wyon family in the same field, and of the ostentation of the Italian in signing his name in full on both sides of certain of the coins.

The Art Union of London which, in the event, proved financially to be a reasonably successful venture, was wound up in 1912.

By that time interest in the medal had declined. The picture postcard had appeared, and the education of an increasing number of the population had encouraged the spread of newspapers. Journals such as the *Illustrated London News,* with its wonderful on-the-spot drawings of events as they happened were flourishing and their scope was now being extended by photography. With such competition the medal returned to its rightful place as an art form. The more accomplished artists' work came into recognition though medals were struck in lesser numbers. Medals began to be struck by and for people and organisations who really wanted something permanent, of first class artistic merit and slightly exclusive. Medal societies began to be formed and something of this will be told in a moment.

THE MEDAL IN THE TWENTIETH CENTURY — ITS RETURN TO AN ART FORM

CHAPTER 4

THE MEDAL IN THE TWENTIETH CENTURY — ITS RETURN TO AN ART FORM

NUMISMATICALLY THE twentieth century in Britain started in a very tidy way. One almost feels that Queen Victoria might have wished it so. Her death in January 1901, after sixty-four years on the throne—the longest reign in British history—called for a new coinage, which appeared in 1902. The Royal Mint produced an official Coronation Medal in two sizes and three metals, gold, silver and bronze to mark the commencement of the reign of Edward VII (1901–10) and these were readily taken up by collectors and the general public. Designed by de Saulles they are, save for the gold, common enough today, but should be included in the cabinet of any serious student-collector. Numerous coronation medals were also struck privately.

To mark the coronation of the next king, George V (1910–36) a very fine Coronation Medal was struck by the Royal Mint in gold, silver and bronze, and in two sizes. Looking back now, sixty odd years after the event, one can only marvel at the opulence of the thick chunk of gold that was used for the larger medal.

Almost before the reign had got under way, World War I, that bitter conflict which Edward VII had tried in his own way to prevent, burst upon Europe and finally engulfed most of the civilised world. There was now ample opportunity for the production of medals on a large scale.

In Germany, whose government might better have applied the metal to throw against the Allies in the form of shells, many medals were struck. Large numbers of them, of the extreme propaganda type, came from the hand of Karl Goetz. They were so satirical as to be almost frightening—so twisted by his interpretation of Germany's hatred. His work was no less bitter on the subject of the conditions in Germany after its defeat. As a loyal German, Goetz naturally felt that his country's cause was worthy of his support. In the event the way in which he interpreted this support twisted one who might have been a great medallic artist into the designer of metallic nightmares.

In Britain little metal was wasted on propagandist medals. There was an opportunity, similar to that which occurred during the reign of Queen Anne (1702–14) to use the medal in this way, but it was not taken up to the extent that it was in Germany. The Allies had better things to do with their metal, frequently imported into Britain through the U-boat screen. With all her power concentrated on survival, on the defeat of the aggressor and on the honouring of international commitments, it was not until an uneasy peace had been secured that Britain had time, money and metal to strike more than a few medals.

Of the medals which did appear many were, as one might expect, of the propaganda type. The only one issued in great quantity, and in very base metal, was the famous copy of the German medal struck to mark the sinking of the *Lusitania* in 1915. Both the German and the British versions were pure propaganda medals, in the design of which art played little part. The British version was issued by that department which would now be known as the Ministry of Information, and was intended to show how ruthless the enemy could be in sinking an unarmed passenger liner, plying its normal course from the USA to Britain. The Germans alleged that the *Lusitania* was carrying shot and shell, and that aeroplanes were stowed under tarpaulins, on the forward deck. So far as the author knows this has never been confirmed or denied, though it would appear possible; compare the pictures of 'merchant' ships carrying Soviet rockets under tarpaulins to Cuba during the crisis of 1962 which the late President Kennedy managed to solve.

Private enterprise, with its own financial resources, took a hand in medallic commemoration of some British victories in World War I. *British Naval Medals* by the late Admiral the Marquess of Milford Haven, published in 1919, lists medals marking victories at sea; and examples can be seen in the National Maritime Museum at Greenwich which has an outstanding collection.

During the remainder of the reign of George V, there were relatively few important medals struck when compared with the output during the eighteenth and nineteenth centuries.

A further point should be made here. This book does not take into account medals awarded by such institutions as the Royal Society, the Royal Numismatic Society, the Royal Geographical Society, the Institution of Mechanical Engineers, and many similar bodies. These give medals, often supplemented with grants of money, as awards for original research and scholarship in their respective fields; but these medals, for personal merit, have not so far been of interest to the collector. Medals issued by such societies usually take the same form each time they are struck and they are, in fact, quite rare. They can be an annual, biannual or once-only issue, and are awarded to a single person or to a group of persons. Of the latter type was the medal struck by *The Times* for presentation to those who first flew over Mount Everest in 1933, twenty years before it had been conquered on foot. Only twelve of these medals were struck, of which ten were awarded.

Such medals are magnificent in their splendid isolation. They take the personal award back to its origins and one would hope that they may long continue. It seems certain that they will. Only a few years ago the proprietors of the Snowdon Mountain Railway, almost the last steam-operated railway of its type, which happily prospers as a living museum-piece and a tourist attraction, commissioned one single medal in gold for presentation to Lord Snowdon. Such fine examples make their contribution to the medal as an art form. Their production was not prohibited during World War I, but for gold in some cases silver-gilt was substituted.

The Silver Jubilee of King George V, 1935, was marked by another Royal Mint medal, in two sizes and struck in gold, silver and bronze. It was well received by collectors and by the general public. The gold specimens are now rare. There were also a number of privately struck medals to commemorate the Jubilee, and most of these are now scarce.

There was no official medal struck to commemorate the death of George V, which occurred so soon after the celebration marking his life of service to his country. A few private medals were struck by way of memorial. Some of the dies which had been cut for the obverses of the private Jubilee medals were now used to provide the obverses of some of the memorial medals. Such memorial medals are now scarce: how scarce the collector has yet to realise.

The short reign of Edward VIII, from 20 January till 11 December 1936, posed a problem for the Royal Mint as well as for the private medal strikers. At the Mint dies were prepared for the new coinage and possibly for coronation medals. So far as the coinage was concerned the obverse dies with the king's portrait had to be scrapped, but the work done on the reverse designs appears to have survived in part.

Certain private mints had already gone into production with medals to mark the coronation, and a few of these medals were actually struck. It may not be appreciated by collectors that they are now quite rare. Examples have been seen in silver and bronze, and a few in gold may also exist. For the serious collector they are certainly items that should be acquired, if they can be found.

A point of precedent should be stated here. After the death of a British king the coronation of the next monarch does not take place for at least a year. Thus there is time to prepare new coinage—which has to be announced by Royal Proclamation to

MEDALS IN THE TWENTIETH CENTURY—RETURN TO AN ART FORM

make it legal—and dies for the official coronation medal. A number of selected and officially approved portraits of the new monarch are prepared and private medal strikers may use any of these which they may prefer. The use of a 'freelance' portrait is frowned upon.

When George VI (1936–52) came to the throne in the place of his elder brother Edward, new obverses for the coinage and new permitted portraits for unofficial coronation medals had to be prepared. Edward VIII would have been crowned in May 1937, but as he abdicated in December 1936 and as the coronation date, 12 May 1937, was still maintained, there was little time for all the numismatic preparations.

While most of the obverse dies for coronation medals of Edward VIII had to be scrapped, some survived for the striking of medals which recorded his accession to the throne, even his coronation as stated above, and his abdication. There are in fact quite a number of varieties of such medals in existence. The complex numismatic history of Edward VIII has just been written by G. P. Dyer, Librarian and Curator of the Royal Mint, an admirable, concise record (published by H.M. Stationery Office).

The usual Royal Mint Coronation Medal marked the official beginning of the reign of George VI. Following so closely on the official Jubilee Medals of George V and the accession/abdication medals of Edward VIII, they were readily taken up by collectors and the public. Among private medal strikers some of the reverses for Edward VIII were brought into use for medals of George VI. The most obvious was that showing the Western Towers of Westminster Abbey, where our coronations have taken place for many centuries. This design was suitable to any coronation. Here again the unofficial coronation medals are reasonably scarce.

During the reign of George VI there was a steady but restrained output of medals, never on the scale of the eighteenth and nineteenth centuries. The medal was still on its way back to an exclusive art-form. World War II (1939–45) coming so soon after the king's accession had much the same effect on the medal in Britain as had World War I, but this time neither side had energy to spare to commemorate it in medals.

On the accession of Queen Elizabeth II in 1952 and her coronation in 1953 a long tradition was broken. The Royal Mint produced no official Coronation Medal. With hindsight, this was an error on the part of the Mint. Though Britain was putting a brave face on postwar events, with the Festival of Britain in 1951—not marked by an official medal—and a truly regal coronation for the new queen, the country was in fact still suffering from the great economic sacrifices of two world wars, from the gradual breaking up of the nineteenth-century British Empire and from the dissolution of the Commonwealth of Nations into which the Empire had been turned by the Statute of Westminster of 1931. It was felt that an official coronation medal would not be appreciated. In the event this could have been wrong.

The place of the longstanding official Coronation Medal was taken by a Coronation crown piece, struck in cupro-nickel. It was at once popular and was taken up by collectors and the general public to the extent of 5,962,621 specimens, plus 40,000 proof pieces. Proof sets of the whole of the new coinage of 1953, containing this crown, were offered by the Royal Mint and were over-subscribed. These sets are now rare. Even the currency pieces from halfcrown to farthing, with the crown added, offered in plastic 'sandwich' cases by Spink & Son, who thought up the idea, were quickly sold out. They are now rare. The Royal Mint itself, finding such a demand, offered the currency pieces, without the crown, in a plastic envelope. These too were rapidly absorbed and now command a premium price, in part due to the fact that the envelopes contained the bronze Penny. This denomination failed to appear again till 1961, though this was not to be known in 1953.

This small digression into coinage history has been made because it would appear, on the evidence so produced, that had an official coronation medal been struck it would have been readily accepted and would have made money for the Mint, and so for the country as a whole.

The decision not to strike a coronation medal in 1953 seems to have neglected one point. The Festival of Britain of 1951, for which a special crown piece was struck in a temporary Branch Mint on the Festival site, and for which a limited number of proof sets of the whole coinage was offered, had attracted a large number of visitors from abroad who took up both numismatic offerings with avidity. The point which was neglected was that Britain was now firmly on the world tourist map. Air travel, making little of time and distance, was bringing about a world travel explosion and tourists were discovering in ever-increasing numbers what Britain has to offer in history, art, culture and natural scenery. The British Isles are a world in miniature and this the new generation of world travellers was discovering.

The unofficial coronation medals which were struck in considerable varieties by private enterprise were bought in considerable numbers and found their way into collectors' cabinets and into the hands of souvenir buyers from all over the world. Their rarity has yet to be assessed.

By the early 1950s, therefore, the medal had recovered its popularity in Britain. Now re-established as an art form, it was about to become an investment.

The true collector is frequently not interested in the medal as an investment. Fortunately the commercialisation of the medal in the mid twentieth century did not destroy its artistry. As more and more private strikers jumped on the investment band-wagon, some pretty poor art appeared, but equally a number of first-class artists designed medals of fine quality. Both must be taken into account by the collector, who will soon appreciate the better work.

It took the death of the world's greatest statesman and leader, Sir Winston Churchill, really to set the investment wheels in motion. Spink & Son produced a memorial medal with a fine portrait by the late Frank Kovacs on the obverse and a reproduction of one of the world's most inspired cartoons, by the late Sir David Low, on the reverse. This cartoon, which had appeared in the *Evening Standard* at the time of the Dunkirk retreat in 1940, showed Churchill, alone on the British south-coast shore, shaking his hand in defiance at the oncoming Nazi hordes and saying—'Very well, alone'.

Struck in limited numbers in gold, and in larger numbers in silver and bronze, this medal was itself an inspiration in its conception. Produced at a moment when the world still appreciated the greatness of Churchill, its limited numbers in gold reached a premium price within twenty-four hours, while in silver and bronze it was bought in great numbers throughout the world. Though a commercial venture, as must have been so many commemorative medals far back in medallic history, it sparked off a twentieth-century revival of interest in medals and large numbers of commemoratives, on any and every subject, began to appear.

Thus, Westminster Abbey, faced with the heavy costs of maintaining a deteriorating fabric, and with the 900th year of its foundation just coming up, commissioned a medal to mark the latter event. It was struck by the Royal Mint, which considers it to be one of the finest of its productions in this field in recent years. The Abbey sold limited numbers of this medal sufficient to make a significant contribution towards the cost of keeping in being what is probably Britain's most important building. On the art side, one of the best of modern medals had been struck.

Let us try to look at the commercialism dispassionately. We do not now know how much money was raised for the government, or for private interests, by the sale of the large numbers of medals struck during say, the reign of Queen Anne, when so many were put on the market. It is probably true to say that the medal is basically a commercial proposition and this fact the collector must accept. While his opposite number the coin collector is busy amassing and studying a numismatic art form that was issued of necessity, the medal collector is dealing with a

MEDALS IN THE TWENTIETH CENTURY—RETURN TO AN ART FORM

commercial art form—one which has made a considerable contribution to numismatic art. In fact many of the artists who designed coins were also designers of medals, as a brief glance through Forrer's *Biographical Dictionary of Medallists* will show. Today artists of the standing of Christopher Ironside, Arnold Machin, Frank Kovacs and Paul Vincz have designed both coins and medals.

While some hard words have been said on the subject of medals struck for profit in the second half of the twentieth century, there is no precedent for such criticism. There is only lack of knowledge on the part of the critics. Medals have been bought and sold and struck for profit for hundreds of years. Only on special occasions were they given free. At some coronations, the last being that of George IV (1820–30), medals were thrown to the spectators who crowded the coronation processional route. In our own time medals were distributed free when the Cunard liner *Queen Mary* was commissioned, and by the London, Midland & Scottish Railway to commemorate the centenary of its ancestor the London & Birmingham Railway, 1838–1938.

So the commercial or non-commercial angle should have no influence on the medal collector. He must accept that the medal, even as an art form, is commercialised, just as most of the pictures hung on the line at Burlington House each year are painted by artists who offer them for sale. The medal collector takes the view that his purpose is that of tracing history, or such areas of history as may be of interest to him through the artistry of the medal. He builds up his collection in the pursuit of knowledge and with pleasure in mind, while still keeping an eye on what he is spending, both from the point of view of insurance and of the value of the collection as an asset, a long-term investment put together with knowledge and care.

THE MEDAL OVERSEAS

CHAPTER 5

THE MEDAL OVERSEAS

UNTIL NOW our study of the medal has been confined to Britain. At this point let us turn our attention overseas.

It has been noted that a period of decline in artistic merit took place in Britain during the commerical production period of medals in the eighteenth and nineteenth centuries. (Though a complete catalogue of the later medals struck during this period does not at the moment exist, one is in preparation.) It has also been noted that in the twentieth century the medal in Britain recovered its artistry and popularity.

In the main this picture is not true of Europe, where the medal went steadily on, as one might say, being appreciated as an art form and as a collector's piece, and well catalogued—particularly in Austria, France, Holland, Italy and Poland. The medal has been officially sponsored by the government mints in Austria, Spain and France. A glance can now be taken at some of the medals produced in France—simply taken as an example—during the last few years.

In France there exists 'Le Club Français de la Medaille' which issues a *Bulletin*, dated from its headquarters at l'Administration des Monnaies et Medailles in Paris. This is, in fact, the Mint of France. Imagine anyone having the temerity to suggest that a medal society should be set up at the Royal Mint on Tower Hill.

It could be said that such studies as Le Club Français promotes are left in Britain to the Fellows and Members of the Royal and British Numismatic Societies. Such societies exist also in France but that does not prevent the French Mint from taking the lead in the co-ordination of the study and production of the medal. The same observations can be made about many other European countries.

The *Bulletin* of the Club is produced on a lavish scale. Though bound in limp card covers—typical of continental publishing of this type—it is on fine art paper and its illustrations and typography are of a high standard. It is eagerly awaited, carefully studied and finally added to the libraries of the more important museums in Britain.

The *Bulletin* does not confine itself to the study of modern medals, though these predominate simply because medal striking in Europe is a very popular art form. A typical issue contains articles, well illustrated, on 'Fra Pacioli et la Divine Proportion', 'Le Rattachement du Pavillon de Flore au Musee du Pauvre', 'La Monnaie d'Agrigente' and, as a contrast, 'Le Chemin de Fer de Paris a Saint-Germain'. All this does not pass unnoticed by British students and collectors of the medal. In May 1971 the periodical *Coins, Stamps and Collecting* featured 'The History of the Louvre as seen through the eyes of French Medallists'.

Imagine part of the history of the Tower of London, Baynard's Castle, St James's Palace and Hampton Court Palace thrown together and melted down into a story. This would be, roughly, the significance of the Palace of the Louvre in French history, before French monarchs moved their place of residence to Versailles and Fontainebleau. Readers of Alexandre Dumas will form an opinion of the part played by this ancient palace. Originally it was not unlike the Palace of Whitehall: a great collection of miscellaneous buildings, spread over a wide area. Many architects tinkered with it, till finally it became a museum of considerable extent and appeared in its present form.

Much of this history has been recorded in medallic form: the first Louvre of Philippe Auguste (1190–1210), the Colonnades of Bernin (1665), Perrault's first plan (1667) and his second definitive design (1673). (During this latter period London was starting to recover from the Great Fire of 1666.) All these alterations were steadily wiping the medieval Louvre off the map of Paris, just as Montagu House was wiped off the map of London by the building of the present British Museum.

The modern medal in Europe is not primarily concerned with the illustration of history by way of allegory and buxom Botticellian cherubs and ladies. Allegory plays a great part in the design of medals, as some of the illustrations will show. The contemporary medal is busy recording the modern world, sometimes with a simplicity and an intensity that are almost frightening. A glance through the pages of the *Bulletin* will demonstrate this beyond all shadow of doubt.

Some years ago a plain, almost stark medal recorded the gargantuan efforts of the Dutch to rebuild dykes demolished by a North Sea storm, which flooded a considerable part of the land won with infinite toil and engineering skill from the depths of the sea. In this, as in so many other European medals, we can see something of what can be recorded of history in medallic form. How many medals are being struck to record the achievements of British engineers in providing our motorways?

In Europe there also exists, on a wider basis, 'La Federation Internationale de la Medaille'—FIDEM for short—which held its thirteenth Congress in 1969. It also produces an illustrated record of its transactions, a record equally esteemed by those interested in the medal in Britain. It has sponsored thirteen exhibitions of modern medals in various cities of Europe, one of which was staged at the Royal Society of Arts in the Adelphi, London.

In Poland there is the Museum of Medallic Art in Wroclaw. It issues a well illustrated periodical, devoted entirely to the art of the medal.

Some time ago Spink's *Numismatic Circular* published a long series of illustrated articles on the subject of Medals of Actors, Singers and Dancers, and more recently another on Medals of Painters. Both were by the Swedish student, the late Carsten Svarstad. That there were sufficient medals on either subject to promote such a catalogue is surely proof enough of the interest in medallic art in Europe.

Interest in these catalogues came almost entirely from readers in Europe and the USA. What has gone wrong with the medal in Britain? How many medals—or coins for that matter—are exhibited at the annual summer exhibition at Burlington House? While artists vie with each other to be hung on the line at the Royal Academy, where are the medallists? They are there but in so small a minority that the visitors who come to view, year after year, as a majority pass their works almost without a glance. Yet, as has been said, excellent work in the medallic field is produced in Britain. Rarely, sad to say, is it fully appreciated.

Earlier some account was given of the Art Union, its objects and its medals. The necessity for such a body underlined the relative lack of interest in fine medallic art in Britain. It was by no means the last body to be founded to attempt to popularise the medal in this country. Much later 'medal societies' based their appeal for support not only on the artistic but on the investment interest. The success or failure of such societies is outside the scope of this book. It can only be said that in Britain at the present time there is a rising interest in medals—such 'society' medals included—among collectors.

Similar societies have existed in the United States. One of them, the Circle of Friends of the Medallion in Manhattan, published its medals in book-form cases, giving details of them and of the artist who designed them. It produced medals commemorating Henry Hudson, Robert Fulton, Charles Dickens and many more famous men. The Circle of Friends seems to have ceased operation around the time of World War II, and though not yet fully appreciated by the collector, its productions are now rather rare. In years to come they may command a rarity price, depending on the growth of interest in medal collecting both in the United States and in Europe.

In 1930 the Society of Medallists was founded in the USA. It claims to be the only non-profit art medal collectors' organisation dedicated to encouraging the work of American sculptors. In the forty odd years of its existence the Society has issued over eighty medals of a consistently high artistic quality. Membership costs $16 annually and for this members receive about two medals a year to add to their collection. Past issues are also available to members. Illustrated brochures are produced from time to time. There is a general similarity between the Society, the Club Français and the Art Union of London, in that all exist or existed to foster interest in the medal and, to a greater or lesser extent, to encourage eminent artists to design medals that are offered to collectors either in return for their annual subscription or at reasonable prices.

Certain commercial organisations have been set up in recent years in Britain to offer limited numbers of medals to collectors. One of these, the Franklin Mint, is an American based organisation. A London firm, stimulated by the considerable interest in the railways of Britain, is offering a fifty-year commemorative set of medals of railway interest, marking the Railways Act of 1921, which brought into being the four mainline railways in 1923. Here, as in previous cases noted above, the medals in precious metals—platinum, gold and silver—are issued in strictly limited numbers. It is too soon yet to know whether collectors or investors will profit from such ventures.

The author has lectured in Britain on certain aspects of the medal, mainly that of its illustration of the history of transport, and knows that interest is not lacking. What needs to be understood is the purpose of the medal and its wide interest as a recorder of history and as an art form. It is hoped that what has been said so far may give some help in this appreciation.

THE MEDAL AS A COLLECTOR'S PIECE

CHAPTER 6

THE MEDAL AS A COLLECTOR'S PIECE

IT IS important to know how to collect and care for medals, and how to house them. As will be appreciated, when compared with the large numbers of coins which have been struck, the numbers of medals are relatively small. They are also relatively inexpensive, but if collectors interest grows, prices will increase.

Coin and medal collectors are not likely to meet on the same ground. The coin collector is studying a subject that is always contemporary with the period in which it was produced. According to his interests and theme of collecting he takes in economics, archaeology, art, local interest, national history and a number of other wide subjects, all affecting or affected by the coin. The medal collector is primarily interested in the presentation of history in pictorial form. Like the coin collector, he is a breed on his own.

So, first get your medal. This is not difficult. While it cannot be said that many of the coin dealers who sprang into being with the recent increasing interest in coin collecting also carry a stock of commemorative medals, the older established firms certainly do. The three leading firms—Spink, Seaby and Baldwin —have always carried medals as part of their stock, have studied them and have experts on hand to assist the collector.

Spink's have followed the history of the medal for over 300 years, its growth and decline, its spate during the Industrial Revolution, its later lack of popularity and its growing status in the modern world. From Spink's also has come the reprint of the British Museum Catalogue, *The Medallic Illustrations of British History*. From Seaby's will come the catalogue of modern medals, which has already been mentioned. Baldwin's, established in the nineteenth century, also carry good stocks of medals and welcome the rise in interest in them.

Many of the smaller dealers can draw on the stocks of these three firms when they are requested to supply medals for collectors. If the popularity of the medal continues to grow they will probably go out into the field in quest of medals for their own stock.

Before the collecting of coins reached its present popularity and before so many catalogues with approximate valuations of coins were published, it was possible for the coin collector to pick up coins from dealers in miscellaneous antiques. They often had a few coins on hand, but had little knowledge of their value. This gap in a dealer's knowledge has been closed by such coin catalogues, no such catalogue yet exists for the medal. It is, therefore, possible to shop around among the antique dealers and pick up a medal or two at small cost. In doing so the collector should be guided by certain basic rules.

The first of these rules is that of condition. Since the medal does not circulate as does a coin there is no reason why the collector should accept it in anything much lower than mint state —as struck. While the coin collector may have to accept rare coins in less than mint state, for the simple reason that coins pass from hand to hand and thus get worn and damaged—or in the case of modern machine made coins are damaged before they leave the Mint—the medal is struck as a work of art. As such it is usually protected during its lifetime. It may be said therefore that if a medal is seen to be badly worn or damaged, such damage is in many cases deliberate. Holes are bored through medals so that they can be worn as costume jewellery. They can also be damaged by neglect or ill-keeping.

Medals struck in base metals, such as pewter, tin or brass, will often, through neglect, have become black or collected verdigris. Unless of the highest rarity they should be discarded.

The exceptions to this stringent rule are medals struck in

Pinchbeck or similar metals. Pinchbeck metal is, in effect, a cheap form of gilding, overlaid on base metal, produced before electroplating and similar 'clad' metals had been invented. The gilt overlay soon wears away and tarnishes, with the result that medals in this metal, an eighteenth century invention, are by now in almost all cases shorn of their glitter and look rough and ill-used. Excepting such cases the medal should be in mint state.

As a note in passing, the best legacy left to modern life by Pinchbeck, a toymaker of Fleet Street and inventor of the gilded metal that carries his name, is his clock. This still stands at the Church of St Dunstans-in-the-West, Fleet Street, and its giants can be seen striking the hours on its bells with their clubs.

During the passage of time medals struck in silver may have become tarnished and need to be cleaned. The cleaning of coins is questionable beyond certain minor limits. Ill-advised cleaning may add to wear and thus lower condition. It has been stated on very good authority however that the medal was made to be cleaned. As a miniature work of art it should be seen to its best advantage and should therefore be reasonably clean and bright.

Silver medals can be cleaned with household ammonia, applied on a pad of cotton wool. They should afterwards be brushed with a soft silver-cleaner's brush which will not damage the medal but will restore its sparkle. Such cleaning should only be necessary at reasonably long intervals, dependent on the atmosphere in which the medal has been kept. Various household silver polishes should be avoided, since they tend to deposit powdered substances in the crevices of the design and in the lettering of the legend. Such deposits are very difficult to eliminate. Self-evaporating fluids such as ammonia and methylated spirits do not leave any deposit, while the after-brushing brings up the full effect of the metal.

A certain amount of toning on silver is acceptable but this should not be allowed to get beyond the point where it can outline or enhance the features of the design.

Gold medals will not tarnish. They may tone slightly, and

those which have been kept in a velvet-lined fitted case for long periods may pick up a little of the dye, usually red or blue, from the velvet. Strictly controlled this can produce what is sometimes known as a 'steel blue tone' on both gold and silver medals. It should not be allowed, however, to detract from the appearance of the medal. Better that the medal should be bright and clean, with that subtle appearance which gold alone among metals can achieve.

According to the amount of alloy added to stiffen the gold, and according to what this alloy may be, a rich 'old gold' tone may develop over the years. This is worth preserving. In cases where actual dirt is found on the surface of a gold medal it can be removed with a very mild acid, such as lemon juice, the medal being afterwards lightly brushed with a silver-cleaner's brush and all traces of the acid removed.

Bronze or copper medals should, as a rule, not be cleaned. In the hands of the medallist and the metallurgist bronze has attained an appearance rarely to be found among coins in these metals. Many modern bronze medals have a satin-like appearance, with various tone values on different parts of the design. While lacking the richness of gold, such medals can have a stricking appeal all their own, and nothing should be done to alter this. Other bronze or copper medals may have a very high finish and a deep, almost chocolate tone. Any small amount of dirt is usually harmlessly removed by breathing on the medal and then brushing it with a silver-cleaner's brush. Certain humourous schools of thought suggest that this is best done after a well lubricated lunch.

Pewter or white metal medals are much more difficult to deal with. Neglected medals struck in such metals can go quite black and collect so much verdigris that they present a 'rusty bubble' appearance. Not much can be done about this. The collector should avoid medals in such a state unless they are extremely rare, an unlikely event when they are struck in such cheap common metal.

Medals in brass should not really be polished to a full brassy state. They can look quite attractive with a little toning. A little brushing of the type already indicated may well enhance them.

Platinum medals, like gold, will not tarnish and should not need cleaning unless they become dirty. This they should not do unless they have been very carelessly treated.

In all, repeat all, cases, whatever the method of cleaning, nothing harsh such as a nylon brush or any form of abrasive should be used. Soft soap and warm water are used by some collectors to clean gold and silver medals. This combination can do no damage, as long as the medal is completely dried out afterwards on a soft towel.

The next point for consideration is that of housing a collection of medals. The majority of coins can be kept in a coin cabinet, since, with certain minority exceptions, they are small and round. The same is not true of the medal, which comes in many and various sizes. It is usually much thicker than a coin, so that a reasonably standard cabinet cannot be provided having piercings suitable to take a collection of medals. The medal also comes in various shapes: square, lozenge, rectangular, hexagonal or sometimes quite irregular. Housing medals is therefore somewhat complex.

The apparently obvious method of housing a medal collection is to use a cabinet containing a number of plain drawers, not less than 1 inch deep, lined with billiard-table felt. This has its limitations. Though the medals can be laid out in regular lines their various sizes break the overall regularity. Of itself this is not important but, set out loose in this way, they will move about every time the drawer is opened and shut, and the resultant disarray will produce a feeling of disorder. Some collectors may well prefer them this way, but in the main the coin and medal collector has an orderly, perhaps fussy mind, and likes to see his collection set out neatly.

Spanning the plain open trays with horizontal strips of light wooden beading, thin strips of wood, finished and available by the foot-length, will keep each row of medals in line, but then the variation in size becomes apparent. The horizontal strips may be found to be too close together, so that a large medal cannot be fitted into the collecting scheme of arrangement at its correct point, and, conversely space may be wasted in a costly cabinet.

It may have been gleaned from the above that the collector can use the three or four drawers of the conventional bureau desk to house his collection of medals. This he can certainly do, but with more depth of drawer than will ever be needed. Lift-out trays might be obtained stacking one on another and using the full depth of the drawers. They should rest on each other, not on the surface of the medals in the tray below.

An alternative, given such open trays or drawers, is to make or have made a series of cardboard boxes. Based on the size of the largest medal likely to be encountered, say 4 inches in diameter, the boxes are related. The largest box being 4 by 4 inches, four smaller boxes 1 inch square will take up almost the same amount of space. An intermediate size of box, 2 by 2 inches, will stack north-south in the same height but in half the width of the 4 by 4 inch box.

This is about as far as the related-size boxes will adapt to the tray. If such a method of housing is contemplated the size of the tray or drawer into which the boxes will have to fit must be related to the sizes of the boxes themselves. If 4 by 4, 2 by 2, 1 by 1 inch boxes be contemplated, the area of the tray or drawer into which they will have to fit as units must be a multiple of such units. If the open tray or drawer is 13 inches north-south by 30 inches east-west, space on the 4 by 4 multiple will have been wasted. Better to have the boxes on a multiple that will fit the tray or drawer, bearing in mind that medals come in all sizes, not necessarily regular or related to each other.

There are other methods of keeping medals. Since we are, for reasons of comparison, contrasting the medal collector with the coin collector, some of these methods would make the latter shiver with apprehension. It must be realised that, as an art form related to pictures and sculpture, the medal can be put on visual display, while the coin is not expected to be displayed in the same way.

The National Maritime Museum in Greenwich, London, which has the finest collection of medals relating to the maritime history of Britain, dealt with the problem of display and appreciation of the medal in an excellent if expensive manner. The collection is housed in part horizontally and in part vertically.

The medals displayed horizontally are set out on a sheet of glass, with a mirror below. The viewer looking down on the medals from above, sees the obverse directly and the reverse in reflection. By pushing a button artificial light illuminates the display.

The vertical display sets out the medals upright on a ledge of wood cut in a succession of curves which hold each medal in place. They are also poised before a mirror in which the reverses can be viewed. Again light can be turned on so that the whole can be seen to best advantage.

This is an expensive method of display paid for by certain generous donors who were prepared to dig deep into their financial resources to ensure that Britain should have a museum worthy of her splendid maritime history. Such magnificence unfortunately is beyond the pocket of the more humble medal collector.

A more simple and less costly display method is that of the glass-topped show table. This has two levels, and medals set out on the lower level can be seen through the glass of the upper level. Only one side of the medal can be seen—the side the collector feels is of the greater interest. Though in theory the table can be used as such, perhaps as a coffee table, when it is moved around the medals if not anchored in some way will also move around. A confused mass of medals will result and art is not best displayed in a state of confusion.

Medals may also be displayed like pictures on the wall. This can be done quite simply. A deep picture frame with a wooden back covered with felt or velvet can be used to display a small section of a medal collection and enhance the atmosphere of a room. The medals are held in place by three cabinet-pins—even the domestic pin will serve—driven into the wooden background at about 4 o'clock, 8 o'clock and 12 o'clock. The medal is then placed between the three pins, the tops of which are bent over and clipped off to the absolute minimum necessary to hold it in place. Thus secured, the medals will stay in position when the frame is hung on a wall. It need hardly be said that considerable skill is needed in dealing with the clipping off and bending over of the pins if the medal is not to be damaged. Such skill can be cheaply won by mounting a few worthless coins on a plywood background for practice. A very light, well balanced hammer will give considerable help.

If a depression of suitable size, shape and depth, can be cut into the background so that the medal sits in it, so much the better. Once again only one side of the medal can be seen. An alternative is to fit each medal into the cut-out background and then glaze both sides of the frame, the glass being close enough to hold the medals in place. In this way either side of the medal can be seen. The main limitation is that of weight. Medals are usually much heavier than coins so that a large collection cannot be easily displayed in this way, save in many frames. The larger collection is thus forced back into some form of cabinet.

The framing method of display can be taken one stage further. Medals can be set round a map or picture illustrating the story that the medals tell. As an example, many medals were struck to commemorate the Battle of Vigo Bay in the reign of Queen Anne. A selection of these could be set round a map of Vigo Bay, or a picture of the action, and an excellent presentation obtained.

Such wall displays, while colourful in themselves and excellent in their conception, are more acceptable in the museum or the company boardroom than in the home of the private collector. The true medal collector, like the true coin collector, wishes to be able to handle—with care—the various specimens in his collection. He likes to be able to hand them to his friends for appreciation and to study them under the glass at close range to note the finer points of their design. Thus some free form of housing, such as the medal cabinet, is the more acceptable to the true collector.

He is not alone in this idea. The larger collections of medals, such as that at the British Museum, are housed in open cabinets, so that any single specimen can be taken out and studied. Thus we are back with the open tray cabinet, from which the collector may take any medal, savour its touch, study its art and through its art the man who designed it. In whatever way the problem of housing the medal is overcome, it should give maximum protection from damage to each and every specimen.

Quite a number of medals were originally offered in fitted cases. Many modern medals, such as those of the coronations of Edward VII, George V and George VI are still offered in this way. What should be done about these cases is a further problem for the collector. If his cabinet has trays of sufficient depth he may wish to keep the medal in its case, with the general feeling that medal and case belong together. Other collectors may discard the case, which from some points of view is a pity—they are now very expensive to produce.

Many recent medals or sets of medals are offered in such fitted cases. Most collectors prefer displaying case and medal together, and the case does make a fine display background. The cased section of a medal collection can easily be housed in the drawers of a desk or in a commercial cabinet of shallow drawers.

There are, of course, always the odd men out among medals. The author has a uniface piece, 4 inches in diameter, which was made from the lead taken from the roof of Temple Bar, the western gate of the City of London. This gate was designed by Sir Christopher Wren and was removed from its site in Fleet Street in 1878, since when it has stood neglected and falling to pieces on a private estate near Enfield. Various schemes to preserve it and return it to the City have so far proved abortive. The piece is housed in a heavy glass-topped brass mounting and is designed for use as a paperweight. Some $\frac{3}{4}$ inch thick, it would not fit easily into a medal cabinet and is best used for its original purpose. Medals may also be encountered fused into blocks of transparent plastic, designed for a similar purpose.

While most museums have medals as a part of their general collection, these are not always readily available for study. No collector or student of the subject should ever leave a museum, however local, without first asking if the collection contains any medals. The more local the museum the more chance of there being some quite rare medal of purely local interest: do not neglect the chance to discover such medals.

Four museums south of the Scottish border have permanent displays of medals: the British Museum; the Ashmolean Museum, Oxford; the Fitzwilliam Museum, Cambridge; and the National Maritime Museum, Greenwich. Their combined resources are sufficient to keep the collector and student of the medal fully occupied. In Scotland the Hunterian Museum in Glasgow, the Royal Scottish Museum and the National Museum of Antiquities in Edinburgh should be visited.

When travelling abroad, it is safe to assume that the national museums of the principal countries of the world all have medal collections of varying size or importance. Europe in particular is rich in fine collections in cities such as Stockholm, Berlin, The Hague, Amsterdam, Paris, Lisbon, Rome, Milan, Athens and many more. To list all the museums where permanent exhibitions are on view or where medals may be seen would fill a handbook. The simple rule is, where there is a museum, art gallery or similar institution, ask to see the medals.

COLLECTING THEMES

CHAPTER 7

COLLECTING THEMES

SO FAR as this story has progressed the medal collector has frequently been compared with the coin collector. The latter usually builds up his collection on some theme. He has plenty to choose from since coins, as civilisation progressed, were struck in increasing millions. He must therefore fine down his collecting theme to something which interests him by way of history, metal used, design, country, period or some similar consideration.

Though large the medal collector's field is not quite so wide. Even so, he must confine himself and his collecting to some theme in which he finds an interest. Otherwise he will only amass a miscellaneous collection of unrelated medals which will have little interest other than that of displaying various art forms. His collection will have little value as an historical theme, little reward for the collector in the amassing of knowledge and, finally, little financial return as an investment of capital. The author has frequently been criticised for his unyielding stand on two points: fine condition of either coin or medal, and the need for thematic collecting, on however wide a basis. After some thirty-five years in dealing with coin and medal collectors he is as convinced as ever of their importance. During this period he has seen too much good money dissipated by the uninformed on coin and medal collecting, money that could well have produced a fine collection and a good investment.

The following are just a few suggested themes the medal collector may care to consider.

COLLECTING THEMES

PORTRAITURE

The obverse of a medal frequently has a fine if stylised portrait, often of a king or queen or of a person of considerable interest. Many such portraits are by artists who not only designed medals but were also painters or sculptors. They were also often contemporary with the people they portrayed. The bust of Queen Anne on her long series of medals is usually after the Kneller portrait, engraved for medals and coins by Croker. An exhibition of his work held at the National Portrait Gallery in London in 1971 gave some idea of Kneller's contribution to painting.

Many of the medals of William IV are after Chantrey, who is equally well known as a sculptor. A royal bust by this artist can be seen in the National Maritime Museum, Greenwich, since William IV was known as 'our sailor king'. He was in fact the Lord High Admiral and his baton, similar to that of a Field Marshal, rests in the same museum. How William used his appointment is another story, well worth investigating by the collector; it would add colour to this part of his collection.

In the wider field many medals are struck simply as portraits. There are almost 100 medals with portraits of Sir Winston Churchill by eminent contemporary artists. The portrait of a man of such eminence dominates the medal and frequently renders the reverse design of secondary importance.

The study of portraiture can be carried on through sovereigns, statesmen, actors, architects, medical men, engineers and many more. The field is large. The development of the medallic portrait may be studied over some four centuries, or the collector may choose a shorter period more to his liking.

HISTORICAL EVENTS

The reverses of many historical medals show some event of importance. The landing of William III at Brixham, the Battle of Vigo Bay, the taking of Gibraltar—these and many other events are all represented on medals, even though portraits may dominate the obverses. This is a good collecting theme, which may be extended to the medals of other countries.

ALLEGORY

The medal often presents history by way of allegory. This is defined as the description of one thing under the image of another. Thus in the British series the Accession of George I (1714–27) is shown on some medals by the Hanoverian horse leaping the North Sea from Hanover to Britain. This is but a single example among several hundred such allegorical medals in the series.

DIRECT REPRESENTATION OF HISTORY

Many medals of the nineteenth century—for example—show some event of historical importance by presenting a picture in medallic form. The opening of the Liverpool & Manchester Railway is shown in several such direct pictures. Some show trains passing through the great Olive Mount cutting at Liverpool, a great engineering feat in its time, through which the modern passenger travels at such a speed that it passes unnoticed. Others show the first train passing over the Sankey Viaduct. Passengers can be seen in the little train, the ladies with their parasols raised, sitting in open coaches. Family road coaches, mounted on flat cars, are shown travelling with them; a precursor of the modern Motorail car-carrying trains.

Other medals show Robert Stephenson's great Britannia Tubular Bridge, recently destroyed by fire, the first and second Tay Bridges and the massive Forth Bridge whose design was modified after the failure of the first railway bridge crossing the Tay—a reflection as it were of the failure of certain modern bridges now being constructed.

Within this collecting theme lies another—the history of modern mechanical transport. Ships, sailing and steam, from the great steamships of Brunel to the *Queen Mary*; the 'coffin ships' that brought about the Plimsoll line; travel in the air from the balloon to the space rocket; horse-drawn vehicles, bicycles and motor cars—all are represented on medals. The whole history of modern transport can be assembled in a thematic collection.

Many other divisions of the direct representation theme exist to attract the collector. He may easily discover one or more of his own.

ARTISTRY IN MEDALS

Artistry in the abstract is the subject of many medals, particularly in the more modern series, such as those referred to from 'Le Club Français'. The development of pure art as seen through the medal is yet another collecting theme, which will enlarge itself with a little study and reflection.

CONTEMPORARY VIEWS

Not a few medals show contemporary views of towns, often as backgrounds to the main subject. Towns or parts of towns, such as gates and castles, fortifications and town plans, are to be found on medals. The comparison of direct views of towns, then and now, is frequently of interest, particularly now that town skylines are changing so quickly.

As an example, one has only to look down from Hampstead Heath, the heights of Sydenham, Greenwich or Hornsey, to see how buildings that once dominated the London skyline—such as St Paul's Cathedral, the Senate House of the University of London, St Stephen's clocktower (usually wrongly called 'Big Ben') and the Victoria Tower of the New Palace of Westminster (also known as the Houses of Parliament)—have now shrunk into the lower part of a view dominated by our modern tower blocks. There are not many medals showing views of London, more's the pity. Continental artists, given such fine viewpoints as those mentioned, would certainly have made use of them in medallic art, as so many painters have done.

CONTEMPORARY VIEWS OF BUILDINGS

From the view of the city to the view of its important buildings. There are plenty of medals showing buildings; cathedrals and churches, town halls and railway stations, large country houses and the like are frequently used as medallic subjects, sometimes at the time of their completion, or during their period of construction or ultimate ruin.

'Temporary' buildings, such as those that have housed exhibitions and have later been pulled down, moved or altered, frequently appear on medals. One occasionally comes across a medal showing the building used to house an important nineteenth century exhibition in Manchester. One or two medals show some parts of the old 'White City' in West London, others parts of the British Empire Exhibition buildings at Wembley. There is also at least one medal showing Olympia as it was originally built in London, before later additions were made to it.

A very interesting record of the various phases of the Crystal Palace can be built up from medals. The Victoria and Albert Museum, itself stemming from the Great Exhibition of 1851, has a fine collection. Many medals show the Palace as it was designed by Paxton for its original use in Hyde Park. Others show it as it stood, enlarged and flanked by its twin towers, on the hill to which it was moved at Sydenham in South London. One of the first 'prefabricated' buildings, it was an inspiration both in its construction and in its name—a building the Victorians did not want to lose.

High on its South London hill, the building of glass could shine like gold in the sunlight, twinkling in derision at its ghastly counterpart in brick in the north, Alexandra Palace. This latter also commemorated by a medal or two was surely one of the ugliest buildings ever to be constructed. It has recently been improved by the Greater London Council, who removed its unsightly towers. It was the world's first permanent television station. Its site and also that of the Crystal Palace, were they in Rome or Lisbon, would be on the tourist's coach tour, since both have unrivalled views of the mass of London.

Buildings feature on many medals all over the world. Quite a study of architecture and of man's pride in his powers of building can be seen through the medal.

MEDALLIC ARTISTS

As one may collect pictures from the brush of one particular artist, so one may collect medals. Medallic artists are less well known than painters, though some have also been painters or sculptors and worked in various art fields apart from medals.

One example might be given as an illustration, that of Cecil Thomas, whose initials appear on Britain's 1953 coinage. Though he has worked on the design of coins and medals, his contribution to art is on a far wider scale: he is pobably the last man to cut gems by the old methods, with primitive gem-cutting tools and equipment; he has designed fountains and ceramic tiles. As a sculptor he will long be remembered for his truly inspired statue of Peter Pan, which went to New Zealand in the 1960s. Cecil Thomas did not design coins and medals as a sideline, but as part of his artistic life. The same can be said of many other artists who have designed coins and medals. Their contribution to art is of equal importance with that of pictures and sculpture, and as such is worthy of study and appreciation by the collector.

It has already been pointed out that many of the medals available to collectors in the Henry VIII—James I period of British history were by foreign artists or by artists, such as Dassier, who designed medals covering this period some centuries later. The few artists selected here for comment, therefore, start in the reign of Charles I (1625–49) with Nicholas Briot.

Briot (c 1579–c 1646), of French extraction, was born in the province of Lorraine. He entered the British numismatic story during the period when experiments were being made with milled coins, and left it during the early part of the Civil War, which was to stifle such progress for twenty years. He was chief engraver at the Paris Mint 1606–25, was appointed to the same post at the Royal Mint in 1633, and was mint master in Scotland (which then had its own separate coinage) from 1635 to 1639. He was also the engraver of the coins of Lorraine from 1611 till 1624.

His work on the improved method of striking coins embodied the use of primitive machinery that produced coins of greater regularity of shape and clarity of detail than had been attained by many artists whose coins were struck by the hammer. His work at various European mints—Paris, Nancy, Charleville, Sedan, Verdun, London, Edinburgh, Oxford and York—gave him great experience. His output of medals was very considerable, as also his designs for coins.

Remembering what has been said above about medals showing views of cities, let us take one from among Briot's prolific output. There are two obverse types of this medal, marking the return of Charles I to London after his coronation as king of the then separate kingdom of Scotland in 1633. One shows the king on horseback, the other his bust—a fine portrait. The common reverse shows a view of the City of London, taken from about the point where the modern Bankside power station now stands. Old London Bridge with its buildings, to serve for some centuries to come; old St Paul's, to be burned down 33 years later in the Great Fire of 1666; the spires of churches of the pre-Wren era; all are clearly pictured with the river in the foreground. Collectors should be warned that cast impressions of the first rare type are common, and that the second type is always cast and chased. They are not Briot's best work, but examples that fit into the portrait and city-view themes.

Forrer, in his *Biographical Dictionary of Medallists* says that Briot trained two other great artists, Pierre Blondeau and Thomas Simon.

Blondeau, coin engraver and medallist, was also a Frenchman, and if he received any training from Briot it would have been in Paris. His work in this country consisted mainly in striking coins from his own improved machinery. Apparently he did not strike any medals in Britain, so his story, important as it is in our coinage history, does not concern us further.

Thomas Simon we have already met in connection with Cromwell's Dunbar medal. He is said to have been responsible for the rather dull coinage of the Commonwealth, but to have been more interested in medallic designs than those of coinage, and frequently to have worked from the models of his brother, Abraham Simon. In fact Abraham a colourful character, appears to have been the real artist. He carried round with him a small piece of wax-covered glass, and whenever he saw a face that took his fancy, he quickly modelled it in the wax. With long hair and beard and eccentric dress he excited derision in public but was in fact an excellent artist.

The medallic work of the Simons was carried out mainly during the Commonwealth period. Thomas Simon, who was chief engraver at the British mint from 1649 till 1660, almost lost his position to the Roettiers when Charles II was restored to the throne. He and his brother contributed many fine medals to the British series, but Thomas was dilatory in many respects.

When Charles II returned to Britain he had already promised the Roettier family that he would find positions for its members at his Royal Mint. At the same time it was decided that hammered coinage should be superseded by milled—machine-made—money, and a competition for the designs was held between Roettier and Simon. So slow was Simon in submitting his designs that the king actually wrote to him to try to hurry him up a little. But it is said that, on account of the promise to the Roettier family given by the king, the result of the 'competition' was a foregone conclusion. As a consequence the designs of Roettier were accepted for the new coinage and during the reign of Charles II many fine medals were struck from Roettier's designs. Three Roettier brothers—John, Joseph and Philip—all worked at the Royal Mint during this period, and their medals would form a worthwhile theme for the collector. For a century there were various members of the Roettier family designing medals in various countries of Europe and a collection representing their work could form another interesting study.

It would be possible to follow this, or many other themes, at some length, but it is hoped that sufficient guidance has been given to stimulate the collector's imagination. As an experiment a possible theme of collecting is now set out in Appendix I.

APPENDICES

APPENDIX I

AN EXAMPLE OF THEMATIC COLLECTION
Does the propaganda medal really reflect history?

THEME: Louis XIV of France versus the civilised world. War as seen through the propaganda medal

TIMETABLE OF EVENTS

In France		*In Britain*
Louis XIV born 5 September 1638	1638	Charles I on the brink of civil war
Succeeded to the throne, age 5, 1643	1643	King at war. Siege of York
Died 1 September 1715, age 77; reigned 72 years	1715	Second year of reign of George I (1714–27)

Louis XIV thus reigned during that part of English history covering :—

1. Second part, reign Charles I, 1625–49
2. Commonwealth, 1649–60
3. Charles II, 1660–85
4. James II, 1685–88

APPENDIX I   AN EXAMPLE OF THEMATIC COLLECTION

5   Interregnum period, 1688–89

6   William & Mary, 1689–94

7   William III, 1694–1702

8   Anne, 1702–14

9   George I, 1714–27, till second year of reign, 1715

It will be seen from this timetable that if the propaganda medals of Britain and her allies are to be set against those of France and her allies it is not necessary to take the story as far back as 1643.

At this point it might be well for the collector to read a short history of the reign of Louis XIV—a good brief account is Maurice Ashley's *Louis XIV and the Greatness of France*. The story is too long to be told here. Louis took over the government himself, being a kind of king-dictator (dictators were yet to come). When on 16 November 1700 he placed his 17 year old grandson Philip, Duke of Anjou, on the throne of Spain, the threat to the English and Dutch trade, as to that of the rest of the world, was too great to be ignored.

At this time Spain was at the height of her commercial power, with vast possessions in the Americas and the West Indies. Since France held large parts of North America and Canada, with a coastline on the Atlantic and on the Mediterranean, and influence in the various kingdoms of Italy, the threat was indeed serious. The Mediterranean could be closed to all trade if France and Spain said so. So also could most of the then discovered America.

While there were already a long string of French medals commemorating the Sun King's conquests—one marking the Battle of Rocroy was struck in 1643, his succession year—we can take up the story from the point at which Britain began to be drawn into the conflict. Since we are studying the subject as seen through the medal the result will not necessarily be histori-

APPENDIX I AN EXAMPLE OF THEMATIC COLLECTION

cally accurate. It will be biased by propaganda and generally distorted. It is advisable, therefore, for the collector to do a little reading, perhaps of Ashley, and of the period as seen through the eyes of the British historians. So to our theme of collecting.

The build-up towards the War of the Spanish Succession began as far back as 1658, during the Commonwealth. The two columns below will set out the actual medals struck. The first are French medals, the second the related medals struck in Britain or included in *Medallic Illustrations* as part of British medallic history though struck abroad.

The medals of France are taken from *Medailles sur les principaux événements du regne de Louis le Grand* 1702, and are given by folio number. The medals of Britain are taken from *Medallic Illustrations of the History of Great Britain and Ireland to the death of George II,* and are given by volume, page and serial number, viz 1, 300, 17–29. Both books contain considerable historical notes, which are most helpful to the collector not only in filling in the background but also in showing the propaganda bias.

	FRANCE	BRITAIN
1658	Battle of the Dunes, 48	Battle of Dunkirk, 1, 425, 67–70
	Capture of Dunkerque, 49	Dunkirk taken, 1, 429, 72–73
	On this occasion the British were fighting with the French against Spain	
	Capture of Mortare, 51	
	Capture of several towns, 52	
1659	Peace Conference, 53	
1660	Fortification of Marseilles, 54	
1661	King takes over government of the State, 59	Coronation of Charles II, 1, 427, 76–85

APPENDIX I AN EXAMPLE OF THEMATIC COLLECTION

1662	Acquisition of Dunkerque, 71	Cession of Dunkirk (for 5 million livres), 1, 497, 126–136
1663	Capture of Marsal, 75	
	Alliance of the Swiss, 76	
1664	Battle of St Gothard, 78	
1666	Assistance given to the Dutch, 89	Alliance of France and Holland, 1, 514, 157–9
	English driven from St Christopher, 90	Island of St Christopher, 1, 517, 163
1667	Campaign of 1667, 95	
	Capture of Tournay and Courtray, 96	
	Capture of Douay, 97	
	Capture of Oudenarde, 98	
	Capture of l'Isle, 99	
1668	Capture of Besançon, 104	
	Capture of Dole, 105	
	Conquest of Franche-Comté, 106	
	Peace of Aix-la-Chapelle, 107	Suspension of hostilities between France and Spain, 1, 543, 197
	Franche-Comté restored to Spain, 108	
1670	Conquest of Lorraine, 115	
1671	Fortification of Dunkerque, 117	
1672	Campaign in Holland, 120	
	Four towns on Rhine taken, 121	
	Naval Battle, 122	Battle of Solebay, 1, 551, 209–10
	The Rhine crossed, 123	
	Dutch forced to abandon their entrenchments on the Issel, 124	

APPENDIX I AN EXAMPLE OF THEMATIC COLLECTION

	Conquests of the king in Holland, 125	
	Capture of forty towns, 126	
	Sacking of Woerden, 127	
	Lifting of the siege of Charleroy, 129	
1673	Elector of Brandenbourg pushed back to the Elbe, 130	
	Capture of Maestrick, 131	
1674	Second conquest of Franche-Comté, 132	Peace of London (between England and Holland), 1, 561, 225–8
	Capture of town and citadel of Bensançon, 134	
	Capture of Dole, 135	
	Battle of Sintzheim, 136	
	Battle of Ladenbourg, 137	
	Battle of Senef, 138	
	Defeat of the Dutch in America, 139	
	Raising of the Siege of Oudenarde, 140	
	Battle of Ensheim, 141	
1675	German army driven from Alsace and forced to re-cross the Rhine 143	
	Sacking of Messine, 144	
	Capture of Huy and Dinant, 145	
	Capture of Limbourg, 146	
	Battle of Altenheim, 147	
	Campaign of Catalogne, 148	
	Raising of the siege of Haguenau, 149	

APPENDIX I   AN EXAMPLE OF THEMATIC COLLECTION

1676   Naval Battle of Agosta, 152
       Capture of Condé, 153
       Capture of Bouchain, 154
       Naval Battle of Palerme, 155
       Capture of Aria, 156
       Raising of the siege of Maestrick, 157
       Recapture of the Isle of Cayenne, 158
1677   Battle of Tobago, 159
       Capture of Valenciennes, 160
       Battle of Cassel, 161
       Capture of Cambray, 162
       Capture of St Omar, 163
       Defeat of the Spanish in Catalogne, 164
       Raising of the siege of Charleroy, 165
       Capture of Fribourg, 166
       Capture of the Fort of Tobago, 167
       Capture of St Guislain, 168
1678   Expedition to (of) Gand, 169
       Capture of Gand, 170
       Capture of Ypres, 171
       Capture of Lewe or Leau, 172
       Capture of Puycerda, 173
       Campaign in Germany, 174

APPENDIX I AN EXAMPLE OF THEMATIC COLLECTION

	Peace of Nimegue, 175	Peace of Nimeguen (between France and Holland), 1, 572, 243–4
	Battle of St Denys, 176	
1679	Peace of Nort, 178	
1680	Reduction of ten towns in Alsace, 179	
	Fortifications of Hunningue, 185	
1681	Reduction of Strasbourg, 186	
	Citadel of Casal returned to the king, 187	
	Strasbourg subdued and Casal returned, 188	
1683	Fortification of Strasbourg, 195	
	Bombardment of Algiers, 196	
	Capture of Courtray and Dixmude, 198	
1684	Bombardment of Genes, 202	
	Capture of Luxembourg, 203	
	Peace with Algeria, 204	
	The Truce (for twenty years), 205	
1688	Capture of Philipsbourg, 222	Landing of William of Orange, 1, 637, 61–7
	Campaign of the Dauphin in Germany, 223	
	Forty galleys at Marseille, 224	
1689	Capture of Campredon, 227	

APPENDIX I AN EXAMPLE OF THEMATIC COLLECTION

1690	Battle of Fleurus, 228	Battle of Fleurs, 1, 707, 118–19
	Naval Battle, 229	Action off Beachy Head, 1, 709, 126–7
	Battle of Staffarde, 230	
	Three Battles Won, 231	
	Fifteen galleys at sea, 232	
	Conquest of Savoy, 233	
	English fleet repulsed in Canada, 234	Quebec attacked, 1, 723, 150
1691		Congress of the Allies (to arrange future proceedings against Louis), 2, 15, 181–5
	Capture of Mons, 235	Capitulation of Mons, 2, 20, 187–190
	Capture of Nice, 236	
	Nice and Mons captured at same time, 237	
	Battle of Leuze, 238	Liége relieved, 2, 26, 197
	Capture of Montmelian, 239	Coni relieved, 2, 26, 198–9
1692	Capture of Namur, 240	Battle of La Hogue, 2, 51, 243–272
		Namur taken, 2, 68, 273–8
	Battle of Stenkerque, 241–2	Battle of Steinkirk, 2, 71, 279–285
	Battle of Phorzeim, 243	Rheinfels relieved, 2, 78, 291
	Fortification of 150 towns, 244	
1693	Capture of Furnes and Dixmude, 245	Sea fight off Gibraltar, 2, 83, 298–300
	Capture of Roses (Catalogne), 247	Battle of Landen, 2, 84, 301–7
	Defeat of the Fleet of Smyrne, 248	
	Battle of Nerwinde, 249	

APPENDIX I AN EXAMPLE OF THEMATIC COLLECTION

      Battle of Marseille, 250
      Capture of Charleroy, 251
      Splendour of the Navy, 252

1694 Battle of Ter, 254
      Capture of Palamos, 255
      Capture of Gironne, 256
      Defeat of the English at Brest, 257

Expedition to Brest, 2, 95, 317–18
Dieppe bombarded, 2, 96, 319–20
Havre bombarded, 2, 97, 321–24
Huy taken, 2, 100, 325–6
Campaign of 1694, 2, 101, 327–8

1695 Capture of Dixmude and Deinsse, 260
      Dunkerque Garentie du Bombardment, 261

Casale taken, 2, 125, 371–4

Dunkirk bombarded, 2, 127, 375–6
Brussels bombarded, Namur taken, 2, 129, 378–402
Retort upon Louis XIV, 2, 143, 403–5

1696 Dutch fleet defeated in sight of Texel, 263
      Campaign of 1696, 264
      Peace of Savoy, 265

Assassination plot (of William III paid for by Louis XIV), 2, 150, 413–16

1697 Capture of Ath, 266
      Capture of Barcelona, 267
      Capture of Carthagena, 268
      Barcelona and Carthagena taken in the same year, 269

Successes of Louis XIV, 2, 158, 428

APPENDIX I AN EXAMPLE OF THEMATIC COLLECTION

		France always victorious, 270	Negotiations for peace, 2, 159, 429
		Peace of Ryswick, 272	Peace of Ryswick, 2, 160, 431–93 etc.
1698		Camp of Compiegne, 277	
	1698	First Partition Treaty, 2, 197, 510	
	1699	Treaty of Carlowitz, 2, 200, 513–14	
	1700	Second Partition Treaty broken, 2, 210, 530–2	
1700		Union of France with Spain, 286	

At this point, 16 November, Louis XIV succeeded in placing his 17 year old grandson, Philip, Duke of Anjou on the throne of Spain.

In March 1702 William III died and was succeeded by Anne (1702–14).

Here the French record of medals terminates. The events of the War of the Spanish Succession can be followed in part in *Medallic Illustrations* as will be seen.

1702

Mistrust of Louis XIV, 2, 231, 12

Declaration of War with France and Spain, 2, 232, 13

Nimeguen relieved, 2, 233, 15

Expedition to Vigo Bay, 2, 235, 17–25

Capitulation of towns on the Meuse, 2, 241, 26

Duke of Marlborough, Commander in Chief, 2, 243, 29

APPENDIX I AN EXAMPLE OF THEMATIC COLLECTION

1703   Bonn taken, 2, 245, 33–4
                               Cities captured by Marl-
                                 borough, 2, 246, 35–6

1704   Charles III of Spain,
                                 departure for Portugal,
                                 2, 251, 42
                               Prince Louis of Baden,
                                 Battle of Schellenberg,
                                 2, 252, 45–7
                               Battle of Blenheim, 2, 255,
                                 48–62
                               Capture of Gibraltar and
                                 naval action off Malaga,
                                 2, 266, 64–8
                               British Victories, 2, 269,
                                 69–70

1705 Projects of Peace, 2, 273, French lines forced in
        77–8   Brabant and Flanders,
                                   2, 275, 79
                               Successes of the Duke of
                                 Marlborough, 2, 276, 80
                               Barcelona taken, 2, 278,
                                 83–4
                               Barcelona relieved, 2, 280,
                                 86–91
                               Battle of Ramillies, 2, 284,
                                 92–3
                               Battle of Ramillies and
                                 conquest of Brabant, 2,
                                 287, 95–6
                               Victories of Anne over
                                 Louis XIV (etc) 2, 288,
                                 97–102
                               Ostend taken, 2, 292, 103

APPENDIX I AN EXAMPLE OF THEMATIC COLLECTION

1707 Battle of Alamanza, 2, 293, 104–6
John William, Duke of Saxe-Gotha, 2, 301, 114–123
Toulon relieved, 2, 306, 124–5
Lerida taken, 2, 308, 127–8

1708   Attempted invasion of Scotland, 2, 316, 141–7
Battle of Oudenarde, 2, 323, 149–53
Battle of Wynendale, 2, 327, 155–6
Capture of Sardinia and Minorca, 2, 329, 157–8
City of Lille taken, 2, 330, 159–62
Passage of the Scheldt forced, 2, 336, 165
Brussels relieved, 2, 336, 166–8
Citadel of Lille taken, 2, 338, 169–80
Ghent taken, 2, 346, 181–3
Campaign of 1708, 2, 349, 184–6

1709 Negotiations for Peace, 2, 352, 187–9
City of Tournay taken, 2, 354, 190–6
Battle of Malplaquet, 2, 359, 197–201
Mons taken, 2, 362, 202–3
Campaign of 1709, 2, 364, 202–8

APPENDIX I AN EXAMPLE OF THEMATIC COLLECTION

1710   Douay taken, 2, 369, 213–17

                           Battle of Almenara, 2, 373, 218

                           Battle of Saragossa, 2, 373, 219

                           Capture of Bethune, St Venant and Aire, 2, 374, 220–1

                           Successes of the Allies in the Netherlands and of Eugene and Marlborough, 2, 376, 222–3

         Battle of Villa Viciosa, 2, 378, 225–7   Successes of Anne, 2, 380, 228

1711   Gerona taken, 2, 383, 234–5   French lines passed and Bouchain taken, 2, 385, 237

            1712   Congress of Utrecht, 2, 392, 247–50

                     Negotiations for Peace, 2, 396, 251–3

1713   England abandons the Allies, 2, 398, 254–5

            1713   Peace of Utrecht, 2, 399, 256–73

            1715   Death of Louis XIV. Not in *Medallic Illustrations*

            1722   Death of the Duke of Marlborough, 2, 456, 67–8

Thus came to an end the great efforts of the Sun King, Louis XIV of France, to rule or influence the rule of the whole of the European and American world, with all the side issues that were involved.

It cannot be over-emphasised that this is only an attempt to show a possible collecting theme—how medals are used as a

APPENDIX I AN EXAMPLE OF THEMATIC COLLECTION

means of propaganda—and that no true historical account is to be read into this experimental exercise in thematic arrangement. Nor is the list of medals necessarily complete, for only two major works have been consulted. Moreover countries other than Britain and France involved in the making of this part of European history will have medals of their own.

Not a few of the medals listed are rare, extremely rare, unique or only known from contemporary accounts. The latter are minimal. All those that exist can be viewed at the British Museum, the Bibliothèque Nationale in Paris, or at the Paris Mint.

The rarity of some of the pieces should not deter the collector. The majority are not rare and a very representative collection can be put together. Plaster casts tinted to resemble metal can be produced from the very rare pieces if the collector really feels that he must complete his theme, though they cannot be held to complete the collection. Moreover the museums from which such casts would have to come are not obliged to produce them.

APPENDIX II

SOURCES OF FURTHER INFORMATION

As has been pointed out in the text, the standard work on British medals is the BMC *Medallic Illustrations of the History of Great Britain and Ireland to the death of George II,* compiled by Edward Hawkins and edited by A. W. Franks and H. A. Grueber. This was originally published by the Trustees of the British Museum in 1885 and reprinted, with their permission, by Spink & Son in 1969. It is a two volume work, illustrated by a few woodcuts, but fully detailed in its descriptions. It contains an important Introduction to the whole subject, a bibliography of works referred to and a list of the main collections of medals. There is also a comprehensive list of 'Biographical Notices of Engravers, Artists, Etc. with references to their works'; an index of Engravers' Initials, etc. and an Index of Inscriptions, from which a medal can frequently easily be identified by reference to its legend. There is also a General Index. This comprehensive work ends in 1760.

To assist the collector in understanding the BMC an entry from it is given here with explanatory notes. It is taken from Volume 2, page 53, item number 246:

246. Battle of La Hogue 19/29 May, 1692. (a) Bust of William III, r (b) laureate, (c) hair long, in armour and mantle. Leg. (d) GULIEMUS III.D.G.M.BRIT.FRAN.ET.HIB.REX. F.D. (e) Below DISHOECKE.F. (Jakob van Dishoecke fecit) (f)

Rev. (g) Naval Action; in front, a trophy of the arms of

APPENDIX II SOURCES OF FURTHER INFORMATION

England and Holland surmounted by a naval crown on a trident. (h) *Leg.* MAR.BRITANN.PULS.GALL.MDCXCII. (France driven from the British seas, 1692).

1.5 (i) Rapin, xii, 12 (j) Van Loon, IV, 104 (k) MB. AR. (l) Hague, AR. (m) P.H. Van Gelder, AR. (n) Gotha, AR. (p) Munich, AR. (q) Rare (r).

In this particular instance there are no historical notes, since this is one of the many medals on the same subject (see Appendix 1); but such notes follow the above type of description in the majority of cases.

KEY

(a)   Date given in old and new style. For explanation see Cherney, *Handbook of Dates for the Students of English History,* Royal Historical Society (1948), 10–11.
(b)   William III is facing right.
(c)   He is wearing a laurel wreath, ancient sign of the victor.
(d)   The legend, or inscription on the medal.
(e)   Which translates from the Latin into 'William III by the grace of God of Great Britain, France and Ireland King, Defender of the Faith'.
(f)   The name of the artist.
(g)   Reverse side of the medal.
(h)   A description of the allegorical device as shown.
(i)   The diameter in inches.
(j)   Reference to the same medal in the Rapin Catalogue.
(k)   Reference to the same medal in the Van Loon Catalogue.
(l)   Reference to the specimen in the British Museum collection in silver. AR = silver.
(m)   Reference to the specimen in the Hague collection in silver.
(n)   Reference to the specimen in the Van Gelder collection in silver.
(p)   Reference to the specimen in the Gotha collection in silver.
(q)   Reference to the specimen in the Munich collection in silver.

APPENDIX II SOURCES OF FURTHER INFORMATION

(r) The degree of rarity. Could be 'not rare', 'not uncommon', 'very rare', 'extremely rare', and so forth.

There are also eighteen portfolios, usually bound in three volumes, of plates, published between 1904 and 1911. These have not been reprinted but are sometimes available secondhand. While they illustrate all the medals, the text and historical notes are not so full as those in the original two volume catalogue.

For the years after 1760 no similar catalogue exists. As mentioned, one is known to be in preparation and will no doubt be published in due time.

A bibliography of the more important works on medals of the world is contained in the Philip Grierson *Bibliographie Numismatique,* section X, Cercle d'Etudes Numismatiques, Bruxelles (1966), 159 ff. This is an important and selective bibliography, to which the reader is referred.

From this and several other sources the following bibliography has been compiled. In many cases it lists books or other works that include coins, as will be seen from the titles. Also included are a few Papers that have been read before numismatic societies and which are to be found in such transactions as the *British Numismatic Journal,* the *Numismatic Circular* and similar publications. Not a few of the works listed are out of print, but they can be consulted in the reference libraries of the main museums in which the medal collections of the world are to be found.

Alvarez-Ossorio, A. *Catalogo de las medallas de siglos XV y XVI conservadas en el Museo Arqueologico Nacional* (Madrid, 1950)

Andorfer, K. & Epstein, R. *Musica in Nummis* (1907)

Babelon, E. *Les Médailles historiques de Napoleon le Grand empereur et roi* (1912)

Babelon, J. *La médaille et les médailleurs* (1927)

— *Great Coins and Medals* (1959)

APPENDIX II SOURCES OF FURTHER INFORMATION

Baker, W. S. *Medallic Portraits of Washington* (Reprinted 1965)
Basso, A. P. *Coins, Medals and Tokens of the Philippines* (1968)
Bergsoe, V. *Danske medailler og jetons fra 1789–1892* (1893, Plates published in 1897)
Bernhart (Kroha, editor). *Medaillen und Plaketten* (1966)
Bertram, F. *Catalog of Israel's Coins, Currency & Medals*
Betts, W. C. *American Colonial History illustrated by Contemporary Medals.*
Bingen, J. *Les Roettiers, graveurs en medaille des Pays-Bas meridionaux* (1952)
Blanchet, A. & Dieudonne, A. *Manual de Numismatique Française,* 4 volumes of which volume 3 covers *Médailles, Jetons, Mereaux* (1930)
Bostrom, H. J. *Suomen muistorahat,* 2 volumes (1932–6)
Bramsen, L. *Médailles de Napoleon le Grand,* 3 volumes (1904–13)
Breton, P. N. *Popular Illustrated Guide to Canadian Coins, Medals, etc*
Brooke, G. C. & Hill, G. F. *Guide to the Exhibition of Historical Medals in the British Museum* (1924)
Brown, M. D. *Catalogue of Medals relating to the History of Transport* (1968)
Carmichael, N. *Canadian Medal Catalogue* (1957)
Catalogue of the International Exhibition of Contemporary Medals (1911) Exhibition held by the American Numismatic Society, New York
Cochran-Patrick, R. W. *Catalogue of the Medals of Scotland* (1884)
Craig, J. *The Mint* (1953). Contains some references to medallic work at the Royal Mint
Domanig, K. *Die deutsche Medaille in kunst- und kultur- historischer Hinsicht* (1907)
Davis, W. J. & Waters, A. W. *Tickets and Passes of Great Britain and Ireland* (1922). Contains a number of 'fringe' pieces

APPENDIX II SOURCES OF FURTHER INFORMATION

Delaroche, E., Dupont E., & Lenormant, C. (editors). *Tresor de numismatique et de glyptique,* 20 volumes (1834-46)

Durand, A. *Médailles et jetons des numismates* (1865)

Eidlitz, R. J. *Medals and Medallions relating to Architects* (1927)

Farquhar, H. *Portraits of our Stuart Monarchs on their Coins and Medals.* Series of articles from the *British Numismatic Journal* (1917 ff) sometimes available separately bound

Fiala, E. *Katalog der Munzen-und Medaillen-Stempel-Sammlung des K.K. Hauptmunzamtes in Wien,* 4 volumes (1901-6)
— *Munzen und Medaillen des Welfischen Lande,* 11 parts, sometimes in 5 volumes (1906-16)

Forrer, L. *Biographical Dictionary of Medallists, Coin, Gem and Seal-Engravers, Mint Masters &c, Ancient and Modern, with references to their works, BC 500—AD 1900* (1904-30, reprinted 1971). Two extensive abstracts, *Pistrucci* and *The Wyons,* are sometimes available separately
— *Le type de "Britannia" sur les monnaies de la Grande Bretagne* (1907) Contains references to the work of Roettier

Frederiks, J. W. *Penningen* (1947)

Freeman, S. E. *Medals relating to Medicine and Allied Sciences in the Numismatic Collection of the Johns Hopkins University* (Baltimore, 1964)

Friedenberg, D. M. & Roth, C. *Great Jewish Portraits in Metal* (1964). Selected from the Samuel Friedenberg Collection, the Jewish Museum, New York

Galster, G. *Danske og norske medailler og jetons, ca. 1533-ca. 1788* (1936)

Goldscheider, L. *Unknown Renaissance Portraits* (1952). Medals of famous men and women of the fifteenth and sixteenth centuries

Grant, M. H. *Catalogue of British Medals since 1760.* Four offprints from the *British Numismatic Journal.* Lists only, no illustrations. Covers period 1760-1820

Grove, F. W. *Medals of Mexico,* Volume 1, *Medals of the Spanish Kings* (1970). Further volumes anticipated

APPENDIX II SOURCES OF FURTHER INFORMATION

Habich, G. *Die deutschen Medailleure des XVI Jahrhunderts* (1916)

Hawkins, E., Franks, A. W. and Grueber, H. A. *Medallic Illustrations of the History of Great Britain and Ireland to the death of George II* (Reprinted, 1969). Known as the BMC

Hill, G. F. *Portrait Medals of the Italian Artists of the Renaissance* (1912)
— *Select Italian Medals of the Renaissance in the British Museum* (1915)
— *The Commemorative Medal in the Service of Germany* (1917)
— *Medals of the Renaissance* (1920)
— *Guide to the Exhibition of Medals of the Renaissance in the British Museum* (1923)
— *A Corpus of Italian Medals of the Renaissance before Cellini*, 2 volumes (1930)
— *The Medal, its Place in Art* (1941)

Hyman, C. P. *Catalogue of Coins, Coinages and Currency of Australia,* with specimens of Medals (1893)

Jolivot, C. *Médailles et Monnaies de Monaco* (Reprinted, 1970)

Katz, V. *Die erzgebirgische Pragmedaille des XVI Jahrhunderts* (1931)

Kienast, G. W. *The Medals of Karl Goetz* (1967)

Kirschner, B. *Deutsche Spottmedaillen auf Juden* (1968)

Kochs, H. *Gepragtes Gold, Geschichte und Geschichten um Munzen und Medaillen* (1967)

Krause, D. R. *Swiss Shooting Talers and Medals* (1965)

Lamas, A. *Medallas portuguesas e estrangieras referentes a Portugal* (1916)

Lambros, P. *Coins & Medals of the Ionian Islands* (1968)

Lane-Poole, S. *Coins & Medals, their Place in History and Art* (Reprinted, 1968)

Langerquist, O. & Nathorst-Boos, E. *Mynt och Medaljer* (1960)

Lefebure, C. *La frappe en Belgique occupéeo, 1914–1918* (1923)

Lincoln. *Catalogue of Papal Medals* (Reprinted, 1962)

APPENDIX II SOURCES OF FURTHER INFORMATION

Loubat, J. F. *The Medallic History of the United States of America, 1776–1876* (Reprinted, 1967)

Mackay, J. A. *Commemorative Medals* (1970)

Marx, R. *Les médailleurs français depuis 1789* (1897)
— *Les médailleurs modernes, 1789–1900* (1900)

Mazerolle, F. *Les médailleurs français du XVe au milieu du XVIIe siècle*, 2 volumes and plates (1904)

La Médaille au temps de Louis XIV (1970). A magnificent catalogue of an Exhibition held in Paris. Profusely illustrated

Médailles sur les principaux Evénements du regne de Louis le Grand avec des explications historique (1702, 2nd edition 1723)

Médailleurs et numismates de la Renaissance aux Pays-Bas (1959) Exhibition catalogue

Medina, J. T. *Medallas coloniales hispano-americanos* (1900)
— *Medallas de proclamaciones y juros de los reyes de Espana en America* (1917)

Middeldorf, U. & Goetz, O. *Medals and Plaquettes from the Sigmund Morgenroth Collection* (1944)

Milford Haven, Marquess of. *British Naval Medals* (1919)
— *Naval Medals of Foreign Countries* (1921–28)

Mira, W. J. D. *James Cook, his Coins and Medals* (1970)

Moyaux, A. *Les Chemins de Fer, autrefois et aujourd'hui, leurs Médailles Commémoratives* (1905)

Parkes Weber, R. *Medals and Medallions of the 19th Century relating to England by Foreign Artists* (1894)

Patrignani, A. *Le Medaglie Pontificie de Clemente XII 1730 a Pio VI 1799* (Reprinted, 1970)
— *Le Medaglie de Gregorio XVI 1831–1846* (Reprinted, 1970). This author wrote a large number of books, mainly on papal medals

Polak, A. *Joodse penningen in de Nederlanden* (1958)

Pollard, G. *Renaissance Medals from the Samuel H. Kress Collection at the National Gallery of Art* (1967)

APPENDIX II SOURCES OF FURTHER INFORMATION

Raczynski, E. *Le médailler de Pologne,* 2 volumes (1838)
Resch, A. *Siebenburgische Munzen und Medaillen von 1538 bis zur Gegenwart*
Rinaldi, A. *Catalogo delle Medaglia Papali Annuali da Pio VII a Paolo VI* (1967)
Rochette, E. C. *The Medallic Portraits of John F. Kennedy* (1966)
Rondot, N. *Les médailleurs et les graveurs de monnaies, jetons et médailles en France* (1904)
Sandwich, Earl of. *British and Foreign Medals relating to Naval and Maritime Affairs,* 1st edition, illustrated (1937); supplement (1939); 2nd edition (1950). The Catalogue of the National Maritime Museum Collection
Schembri, H. C. *Coins and Medals of the Knights of Malta*
Schwarz, D. *Schweizerische Medaillenkunst* (1955)
Simonis, J. *L'art du médailleur en Belgique,* 2 volumes (1900)
Storer, H. R. *Medicina in Nummis* (1931)
Strong, R. C. *Portraits of Queen Elizabeth I* (1963). Contains references to medals
Suhle, A. *Die deutsche Renaissance Medaille* (1950)
Sutherland, A. *Numismatic History of New Zealand* (1939–40). See part 5, *Medals of New Zealand*
Svarstad, C. *Medals of Actors, Singers and Dancers*
— *Medals of Painters.* A series of articles in Spink's *Numismatic Circular* (1960's)
— *Moderne Fransk Medaljekunst* (1962)
Tourneur, V. *Catalogue des médailles du royaume de Belgique* (1911)
Trowbridge, R. J. *History, Coinage, Paper Notes and Medals of Edward VIII of Great Britain* (1970)
Van Loon, G. *Histoire métallique des XVII provinces des Pays-Bas,* 5 volumes (1732–7)
Weiss, R. *The Medals of Pope Sixtus IV, 1471–1484* (1961)
— *Pisanello's Medallion of the Emperor John VIII Palaeologus* (1966)

APPENDIX II SOURCES OF FURTHER INFORMATION

Welter, G. *Die Reiningung und Erhalting von Munzen und Medaillen* (1970). English translation available as *Cleaning & Preservation of Coins and Medals*

Whitting, P. D. *Coins, Tokens & Medals of the East Riding of Yorkshire* (1969)

INDEX

Acheson, 23
Albert, Prince (Consort), 33
Alexandra Palace, 31
Allegory (theme), 117
America, discovery of, 43
Anne, Queen, 27, 69, 84, 110
Antarctic expedition (1955–8), 39
Antoninus Pius, 19, 53
Armada, Spanish, 23, 65–6
Arras, finds at, 53
Artistry in Medals (theme), 118
Art Union (of London), 37, 77–9
Assinarian Games, 19

Baden-Powell, Lord, 39
Baldwin (firm of), 103–4
Baronet's Badges, 67
Base metals, medals made from, 104
Bath, Order of the, 67
Beaulah, G. K., 78
Belli, Valerio, 21, 63
Berry, Duc de, 56
Bibliography, 143–9
Biographical Dictionary of Medallists (Forrer), 76–7, 91, 121
Blondeau, Pierre, 121–2

BMC (British Museum Catalogue), 61, 64, 67, 70, 104, 141
Brass, medals struck from, 106–7
Briot, Nicholas, 120–1
British Museum Catalogue, *see* BMC
Bronze, medals struck from, 106
Borgia, Lucrezia, 19
Boulogne, cession of, 63
Boulton, Mathew, 29, 74–6
Bower, George, 69
British Naval Medals (Milford Haven), 85
British Numismatic Journal (Beaulah), 78
Brunel, Sir Marc, 29, 74, 118
Bulletin (Organ of Club de Français de la Medalle), 95–7

Calais, 64
Cathedrals, 37, 55
Cellini, Benvenuto, 56
Chantrey, 116
Charles I, 25, 62, 67–8, 120–1
Charles II, 25, 68–9, 122
Churchill, Sir William S., 37, 89–90, 116
Circle of Friends, Manhattan, 98

INDEX

Club Français de la Medaille, 95–6
Colet, John, 21, 62
Collecting themes, 115–23
Colonnades of Bernin, 96
Constantine, 56
Constantius I Chlorus, 19, 53
Contemporary Views (theme), 118–20
Copper, medals struck from, 106
Corbould, Henry, 77
Coronations, 33, 63, 83, 86–8, 91, 111
Coverdale, Myles, 21, 64
Crocker, John, 27, 116
Cromwell, Oliver, 68
Cromwell, Thomas, 63
Crystal Palace, 31
Cunard Steamship Company, 41, 91

Dassier, Jean, 27, 61–4, 67, 70, 120
Da Vinci, Leonardo, 56
Davis, 21
Davis, Joseph, 23
Demetrius, 52
De Saulles, 83
Dickens, Charles, 97
Diocletian, 19
Dunbar medal, 25, 68, 122

Edward VI, 21, 23, 63
Edward VII, 33, 35, 83
Edward VIII, 86–7
Elizabeth I, 23, 64–7
Elizabeth II, 88
Emery, Edward, 23
Eucratides, 51–2
Everest, Mount, 85

Festival of Britain, 89
FIDEM, 97
Flemish-Burgundian medals, 56
'Forlorn Hope' Badge, 68
Forrer, 76–7, 91, 121
Fox, Richard, 63
Franklin Mint, The, 99
Frederick, Prince of Wales (1729), 27
Fuchs, Sir Vivian, 39
Fulton, Robert, 98

Garter, Order of the, 67
George I, 27, 117
George II, 27
George III, 72
George IV, 75, 77, 91
George V, 33, 35, 83–4
George VI, 33, 63, 87
Germany, medals of, 83–4
Gibraltar, 116
Goetz, Karl, 84
Gold, medals struck from, 105–6
Great Britain, SS, 33, 117–18
Grey, Lady Jane, 23, 64

Hardwick, Philip, 41
Henry VIII, 21, 54, 57, 61–2
Hilliard, Nicholas, 23, 67
Historical Events (theme), 116–17
History of British Art (series of medals), 78
Holland, 97
Holtzhey, Martin, 27
Hudson, Henry, 98

Industrial Revolution, 29, 73–80
Information, sources of further, 141–3
Investiture (of Prince of Wales), 35

INDEX

Ironside, Christopher, 91

James II, 25, 68–9
James IV (of Scotland), 21, 62
Janus, 19
John VIII Paleologos, Emperor, 56
Jubilees, 75, 86–7

KIMON, 19
Kovacs, Frank, 89–90, 91
Küchler, C. H., 27, 75

Large Brass Medals (Smyth), 52
Livingstone, David, 39
London, Corporation of the City of, 77
Louis XIV (of France), 27, 69
Low, Sir David, 90
Lowestoft, Battle of, 25
Luder, Jan, 69
Lusitania, SS, 84

McAdam, John, 74
Machin, Arnold, 91
Marlborough, Duke of, 27
Mary I, 64
Mary (Queen of Scots), 23, 64
Medallic Artists (theme), 120–3
Medallic Illustrations of British History, see BMC
Medals: cleaning of, 106–7, displays of, 107–10; museums where well displayed, 112
Menai Bridge, 31
Mercator, Michael, 63
Middlesex County Council, 35
Mills, George, 29
Mint, The Royal, 33, 54, 68, 74, 76, 79, 83, 86, 88, 90, 121
Minton, J. W., 39
More, Sir Thomas, 21, 63

Mudie, James, 72
Muller, Heinrich, 69

Napoleon Bonaparte, 77
National Medals, 77
Nelson, Lord, 75
Newcomen, Thomas, 74
Newton, Sir Isaac, 57
Numismatic Society (British), 39, 75

Olympic Games, 39

Passarowitz, Treaty of, 27
Paul III, Pope, 21, 63
Penn, William, 39
Perrault, 31, 96–7
Pewter, medals struck from, 106
Philip, Duke of Anjou, 27
Philippe Auguste, 96
Pigeon, G. F., 21
Pinchbeck, 104–5
Pisanello, 55–6
Pistrucci, 76, 79
Platinum, medals struck from, 107
Poland, 97
Pollard, J. G., 75
Pope, Alexander, 70
Popery, Restoration of, 64
Portraiture (theme), 116
Propaganda, medals used for, 83–4
Protestant martyrs, 64

Queen Mary, RMS, 41, 91, 118

Renaissance medal, 55–6
Rocket, The (engine), 29, 31
Roettier, John, 25, 122–3
Roettier, Joseph and Philip, 122–3

153

INDEX

Rogart, Emile, 39
Romney, Hythe & Dymchurch Railway, 19

St Quentin, seige of, 64
Saltus, John Sanford, 39
Scythians, 51
Seaby (firm of), 103
Seltman, 52
Shakespeare, William, 21
Shrewsbury, Battle of, 41
Silver, medals struck from, 105
Simon, Abraham, 122
Simon, Thomas, 68, 121–2
Smeltzing, Jan, 69
Smyth, 52
Society of Medallists (USA), 99
Spanish Succession, War of the, 27, 69
Spink & Son (firm of), 35, 37, 39, 73, 88–9, 103, 141
Stephenson, George, 29
Stephenson, Robert, 29, 39, 74, 117
Svarstad, Carsten, 98
Syracuse, victory at, 19, 51

Tassie, 23, 65
Telford, Thomas, 31, 74
Tennyson, Lord, 39
Themes, collecting by, 115–23

Theodoric, 21
Thomas, Cecil, 120
Tolstoy, 43
Tower Bridge, London, 35
Trafalgar, 29

United States, 98–9

Versailles, Palace of, 45
Victoria (Queen), 33, 75, 77
Vigo Bay, Battle of, 110, 116
Vincz, Paul, 37, 91

Watt, James, 29, 74, 76
Wellington, Duke of, 29, 75
Westminster Abbey, 90
White metals, medals struck from, 106
Wiener, Jacques, 37
William and Mary (King and Queen), 68–9
William III, 68–9, 116
William IV, 33, 75, 116
World War I, 35
Wyon, A. B., 29
Wyon family, 37, 77–8
Wyon, J. S., 29
Wyon, Leonard Charles, 79
Wyon, Thomas (Jr), 76
Wyon, Thomas (Sr), 76
Wyon, William, 31, 33, 77, 79